DO
Baptists Believe
In Basic English

Writer:
Roy T. Edgemon

Translator:
Donnie Wiltshire

Convention Press
Nashville, Tennessee

001116248

© Copyright 1990 • Convention Press
All rights reserved

5890-15

Basic English
This book is the text for course 05063
in the subject area Baptist Doctrine
in the Church Study Course

Dewey Decimal Classification Number: 230.6
Subject Heading: BAPTISTS—DOCTRINES

Printed in the United States of America

Discipleship Training Department
The Sunday School Board of the Southern Baptist Convention
127 Ninth Avenue, North
Nashville, Tennessee 37234

(The Basic English edition is a translation into easy-to-read English by Donnie Wiltshire, pastor to the deaf in New Orleans, LA, or for persons who use English as a second language.)

Writer: Roy T. Edgemon
Translator into easy-to-read English:
Donnie Wiltshire

EDITING STAFF—Special Ministries Department
John Cooper
Editor
Mary Ruth Brew
Manuscript Assistant
Peter Kung
Manager, Language Church Development/New Work Section
Bill Banks
Director, Special Ministries Department
DESIGN STAFF
Pam Goodwin
Doris Adams

Contents

CHAPTER 10

About the Author

Dr. Roy T. Edgemon came from Texas. He was a pastor in Texas for 15 years. He worked after that as a missionary in Japan. He later worked for the Home Mission Board. He was director of evangelism planning and consultation. Dr. Edgemon graduated from Midwestern University and from Southwestern Baptist Theological Seminary. Dr. Edgemon also helped 10 churches as their interim pastor while working for the Home Mission Board and the Sunday School Board.

Anna Marie Edgemon is Dr. Edgemon's wife. She is a writer and a teacher. She has been the Bible teacher for 17 state WMU conventions. She has led many different conferences around the world. She worked for 1 summer as a volunteer missionary, teaching at a university in China. Dr. and Mrs. Edgemon have 1 daughter. Her name is Lori Shepard. She is a physical therapist. Lori is married to Douglas Shepard. He works at the University of Texas. Both Lori and Douglas had missionary parents. Dr. and Mrs. Edgemon have one grandson. His name is Nathan Roy Shepard. This book is dedicated to Nathan.

There is a teaching guide in this book. Dr. Arthur H. Criscoe wrote the teaching guide. Dr. Criscoe is the director of the Management Support Group of the Church Training Department. Dr. Criscoe also wrote *The Doctrines Baptists Believe—Teaching Workbook.* Many helpful ideas for anyone who teaches *The Doctrines Baptists Believe* are in this book.

Preface

MY CALLING AND MINISTRY ARE THOSE OF A PREACHER. I have a pastor's heart. I have stood behind the sacred desk each Sunday for more than 35 years. I proclaimed the Word of God to people from all walks of life. I have tried to communicate to people in their present circumstances. I tried to meet their specific needs. I have written this book with the same commitment. I have approached this task not as a theologian writing a textbook but as a pastor addressing his people.

This book, of course, does not deal with *all* the doctrines Baptists believe. Space limitations did not permit me to write all I would like to on the various topics. The book does represent one pastor's perspective on the key doctrines of our faith. For a more comprehensive study, I commend to you the *Disciple's Study Bible,* which systematically traces 25 doctrines through the Bible. My prayer is that you be rooted and grounded in sound doctrine and not be "carried by the waves and blown about by every shifting wind of the teaching of deceitful men" (GNB) that comes along.

Roy T. Edgemon

CHAPTER 1

The Bible:
the Inspired Word of God

*The word of God is alive and active, sharper than
any double-edged sword. It cuts the way through, to
where soul and spirit meet, to where joints and marrow
come together. It judges the desires and thoughts of
man's heart.* Hebrews 4:12 (GNB).

A PERSON IN RUSSIA WROTE A PLAY
SOME YEARS AGO. The play tried to
make fun of the Christian religion. The name of the play was
Christ in a Tuxedo. The play started like this. The curtain went up.
There was a bar in a church building. Some nuns were standing
at the bar. They were wearing their special nuns' clothing. They
were drinking alcohol. They were betting money on games. The
church looked like a bad place filled with bad people.

The most important actor in the play was Alexander Rustavak.
He was a famous Russian actor. Rustavak was supposed to walk
on the stage and start reading a few verses from the Bible (Matt.
5). Matthew 5 is called "The Sermon on the Mount."

The play started. Rustavak walked on stage. He began to read.
But something happened. He could not stop reading. He read
more and more. He could not stop Everyone became quiet. He
read a while and stopped. He raised his hands and said: "Jesus,
remember me when you come into Your Kingdom." The curtain came down fast. The government in Russia never let the play
be shown again. The Word of God had power over people even

when they tried to make fun. God's Word is alive.

The word *Bible* is a good word. People understand that the word *Bible* means God's Word. The word *Bible* is an English word. That word comes from the Greek word *biblos*. *Biblos* means book. The Bible is a book. The Bible is *the* Book. I really like the words *Word of God*. That is my favorite way to talk about the Bible. That is the way Hebrews 4:12 talks about the Bible. Those words have a strong feeling. The words *thus saith the Lord* are in the Bible about 400 times. What God says--that is His Word. The Bible is what God has said. What God said and what God did were written down. That is the Bible.

Many writers in the Bible used the words *Word of God*. Paul wrote, "Accept salvation as a helmet, and the word of God as the sword which the Spirit gives you" (Eph. 6:17, GNB); and Peter wrote, "Through the living and eternal word of God you have been born again" (1 Pet. 1:23, GNB).

The Bible talks about the Bible itself. The writer of Hebrews 4:12 says four true things about the Word of God. We will study that verse. It will help us understand about the Bible.

God's Word: Came from God

This verse tells us many true things. The first true thing in this verse is that the Bible comes from God. The Bible says *Word of God*. It means the Bible comes from God. God worked with people to make the Bible. The Bible has 66 smaller books in it. These books were written at different times. From the time the first book was written to the time the last book was written was many hundred years.

Many people wrote parts of the Bible. Those men wrote on things like paper made from river plants (papyrus) or animal skins (parchment) or maybe even on clay. All those things are true. The Bible is still God's Word. God was giving His Word during all that time. He worked with people to give His word. Working with people really shows that God has always been showing Himself to people. God was always revealing Himself.

The fourth book in the New Testament is called the Gospel of John. The writer of John talks about *logos* (John 1). *Logos* is a Greek word. The Greek word *logos* is written *word* in the English

Bible. John used *word (logos)* as a name for Jesus. That Greek idea of *logos* was well known by Greek people. Jewish people who lived the same time as Jesus also knew it well. The Greek people used *logos* to mean principle or reason. That was an important idea in high-Greek thinking (philosophy). Some wise people who study the Bible today think John was thinking about the way Greek people used *logos* when John wrote about Jesus. That may be right. It is true that Jesus is the greatest "Reason." But John was Jewish. The Greek idea was not the same as the Jewish idea.

Jewish people used the idea of *logos* to talk about God's power to work in history. This idea means that God is doing things in the world and in people's lives. This means that history obeyed what God commanded. God commanded. God spoke. History changed. God spoke. People received blessings. God spoke. Judgment happened to people. God spoke. Miracles happened to people. God spoke His law. God always speaks with power. Nothing can stop God's Word from happening.

John said that Jesus was God's Word. Jesus was God's perfect word for bringing the world back to God. Jesus was God's Word living on earth. Jesus was the way God worked in history. He was God's judgment and blessing. He was God's power. Nothing can stop that Word! Jesus has come. Now things will happen to make the world become what God has planned for the world. A word shows what a person thinks. Jesus shows what God thinks. Jesus is what God is.

Someone might say we worship the Bible. We say the Bible is 100 percent true. Sometimes people do worship the Bible. We must worship God--not the Bible. I do not think many people worship the Bible. Jesus is the Word of God. God spoke His Word. Jesus was living with us. The Bible is the Word of God. God spoke His Word to people. People wrote what God led them to write.

Jesus and the Bible are not the same thing. Jesus makes it possible for us to understand the Bible. The Bible leads people to meet Jesus. Jesus is most important. A Bible with authority does not make Jesus less important. A Bible with authority shows us what Jesus has done. It makes us feel sorry about sin. The Holy Spirit works through the Bible. God is the most important. The

Bible makes us have clear understanding about God. Then we have a right friendship with God.

There are verses in the Bible that show the Bible came from God. Paul wrote, "All Scripture is inspired by God and is useful for teaching the truth, rebuking error, correcting faults, and giving instruction for right living, so that the people who serve God may be fully qualified and equipped to do every kind of good deed" (2 Tim. 3:16-17, GNB). Peter wrote, "No prophetic messages ever came from the will of man, but men were under the control of the Holy Spirit as they spoke the message that came from God" (2 Peter 1:21, GNB).

Peter meant that people did not decide to write God's Word. The Bible is not what people think up (imagine). Do you think people are as honest as God was honest in the Bible? We do not like to show weakness. But the Bible shows how weak the great people of the Bible were. The Bible shows how David sinned. The Bible shows when Noah was drunk. The Bible shows Lot and his problems. The Bible shows real life. It is like looking in a mirror when we read the Word of God. We see what our own life is like. The Bible shows all of life. We will know the right way to think about all of life. We learn the right way to live when the Bible shows all of life. We learn how God made us to live. The Bible makes clear why people do things the way they do them.

I have a friend in Texas. My friend worked for a telephone company. He checked the phone wires. My friend lived a wrong life. He did not care about good things. He was wild. His marriage ended by divorce. He started to think that no one loved him. He was in a hotel in Abilene, Texas. He was thinking about killing himself. He saw a Gideon Bible in the room. He opened it. It said "Plan of salvation. Turn to these Scriptures." He read those verses in the Bible. He got on his knees about 30 minutes later. He said: "God, I know You're alive. I know this Word is true. I know I am a sinner. God, have mercy and forgive me. Come into my life." The Lord came in his life. God changed my friend. I know hundreds of people God's Word has changed. God's Word changes people because God's Word is alive. It helps people with their needs.

We say the Bible is inspired. People say great books and poems are inspired. We believe the Bible is inspired in a different way from great books and poems. Great books have many wonderful ideas. They can help people in many ways. The great books are important. But the inspiration of the Bible is more. We think all of the Bible is inspired by God, not just parts of it. The New Testament is not more inspired than the Old Testament. Jesus helped us understand the Old Testament in a new and more clear way. An important rule for Christians to understand the Bible right is this rule: "The New Testament explains what the Old Testament means." But the Old Testament was the only Bible Jesus and the early Christians had. It was inspired for them. The Old Testament is inspired for us, too. We mean when we say the Bible is inspired that God gave the Bible with right ideas and right words. The words in the Bible are the right words. The ideas are the right ideas.

Someone wrote each book of the Bible. Each book of the Bible was written for a first time. The first time each book was written is called the original manuscript. Many people like to talk about what the original manuscripts were like. We do not now have one original manuscript.

Wise people study old copies of the Bible. They have been able to find almost exactly what the original manuscripts said, word for word. There is some doubt about a few words. We do not know exactly what word was in the original manuscript in a few places. But those words of doubt are few. They are not important words. None of our beliefs (doctrines) are touched by these few words.

The Bible was not written in English first. Now we have Bibles that are in English. The Bible has been translated from other languages to English. We now have many wonderful English Bibles. It does not matter whether you read the 1611 King James Version Bible or whether you read some new Bible in English. Most of the Bibles written in English are fine to read. It is helpful to read good translation of the old languages. All the good translations of the Bible to English win people who are lost. They help people with their needs. They judge wrong people and teach people. Good translations help people give their lives fully to the

Lord Jesus Christ.

Good thinking (logical) helps us see that the Bible came from God. God shows Himself to us. Good thinking helps us see that God would give us His word. He gives words we can depend on. He gives words that have authority without mistakes. His word tells about how He has shown himself. Good thinking helps us see that God gave us a clear word. It tells what is right and what is wrong. It tells what God is really like. It tells how a person is saved. To think God would leave us without a clear written word of truth is not good thinking (not logical). God would not leave people helpless to deal with wrong ideas and false leaders.

Jesus said, "How wrong you are! It is because you don't know the Scriptures or God's power" (Matt. 22:29, GNB). Jesus supported the Word of God. Jesus showed us by His example the Word of God was important. Jesus knew the Bible. He surprised the wise Bible teachers. Jesus went to the Temple as a twelve-year-old boy. Jesus was tempted by the devil. Jesus spoke from memory (quoted) Scripture. He told His disciples, "If you obey my teaching, you are really my disciples! You will know the truth, and the truth will set you free" (John 8:31-32, GNB).

God's Word: The Breath of God

The second truth from Hebrews 4:12 is that the Bible is "alive and active." The writer uses the word *quick* in the King James Version. The word here in the Greek language is *zon*. *Zon* means life. A little while ago we saw *Zon* in 2 Timothy 3:16. That verse says the Scriptures are inspired (God-breathed). The word here in the Greek language is *theopneustos*. The first part of that word *theo* means God. *Pneustos* means breathed. That means that all Scripture is God-breathed.

The Bible in Genesis 2:7 helps us understand what *God-breathed* means. That verse says, "The Lord God took some soil from the ground and formed a man out of it; he breathed life-giving breath into his nostrils and the man began to live" (Gen. 2:7, GNB). Man came alive when God breathed into the man. It is that idea with the Bible. God breathed life into the written Word. No book is like the Bible. People write other books. They feel good about their books. But the Bible is the only book God inspired. God breathed life into it. The Bible is not only words about God working in people's lives. The Bible has its own kind of life. The Bible still breathes today the breath of God.

The Bible can give life to us. It is a living Word. The Bible will lead us in life. The Bible says it will be a lamp to guide us and a light for our path. (See Ps. 119:105.) The Bible promises that we can depend on it. (See Ps. 19:7.) It promises to show us when we are wrong. It helps us learn to live right. (See Prov. 6:23.) And it promises to lead us to the best life of all. This life has God's Spirit leading our spirits. (See 2 Cor. 3:6.) Jesus said: "What gives life is God's Spirit; Man's power is of no use at all. The words I have spoken to you bring God's life-giving Spirit" (John 6:63, GNB).

"The word of the Lord remains forever. This word is the Good News that was proclaimed to you" (1 Pet. 1:25, GNB). Some scientists who dig up old things and study them (archaeologists) found the grave of a man. That man was in the king's family. Many wonderful rich things were in the grave. There were many fancy glass pots (vases). The glass pots were closed with wax. The scientists found seeds inside it. They decided to plant the seeds. They were surprised when the seeds started to grow. Those seeds were closed up for many hundreds of years. They started to grow when they were given water and sunshine. They were alive. God's Word is like that. God's Word comes alive in our hearts when we believe Jesus. The seed came alive in the dirt. You and I became saved by Jesus because the Word of God gives life.

God's Word: Indestructable (cannot be destroyed)
The third true thing seen in Hebrews 4:12 is that the Bible "is alive and active, sharper than any double-edged sword. It cuts all the way through, to where soul and spirit meet, to where joints and marrow come together." Peter wrote that the body is like grass and passes away fast, "but the word of the Lord remains forever" (1 Pet. 1:25). Jesus said, "Heaven and earth will pass away, but my words will never pass away" (Matt. 24:35). Jesus also said, "Remember that as long as heaven and earth last, not the least point nor the smallest detail of the Law will be done away with—not until the end of all things" (Matt. 5:18, GNB).

Sometimes people have tried to destroy copies of the Bible by burning it. Sometimes people have burned people who tried to write the Bible in the languages people could read. Some people have tried to take out parts of the Bible they did not like. Some nations and governmental leaders have tried to remove the Bible from their countries and from the earth. But now almost every home in America has a Bible. The Bible has been written in many languages. The Bible is all over the world. Many changes have happened around the world because of the Bible. We must see that God takes care of the Bible.

God's Word is strong. It will never end. It will continue until the end of the world. It is like a sword. It is sharp on both sides of the blade. One type of sword was short when Jesus lived on earth. It had a point and both sides of the blade were sharp. It could cut both ways. God's Word is like that in our lives. It is like a sharp sword. The Bible cuts into your soul when you read it. It cuts us with conviction. This happened on the Day of Pentecost when Peter preached. The people shouted out under conviction of sin, "What shall we do, brothers" (Acts 2:37, GNB). God's Word cuts us deep inside our soul. It helps us see what is right and wrong. God's Word makes us see clearly our real lives. It makes us wake up to what God wants us to become.

Revelation 19:13 pictures Jesus coming back to earth at the end. Revelation talks about Jesus with His robe dipped in blood. A sharp sword came from Jesus' mouth. He used the sharp sword to cut down the nations. You will see in that verse what He is called. He is called the Word of God.

God's Word: Convicting Power
The fourth true thing in Hebrews 4:12 is that God's Word judges us. Hebrews 4:12 says that God's Word "judges the desires and thoughts of man's heart." The Greek language word for *judges* is *kritikos.* This is the only place in the whole Greek-language Bible that has this exact word. The English word *critic* comes from this Greek-language word. The idea of this word is that the Word of God looks into our lives. It watches us. It finds what is right or wrong, what is good or bad. God's Word criticizes our lives. The Word of God becomes a judge against our

lives. Someone may feel when it is time to stand before God the Judge, he can say: "Lord, You must understand. I lived in the 20th century. My time is the 1990s. People in my time did not believe what the Bible said about right and wrong." All people must know that God will not judge us by our family or by the years we lived. He will judge us by the living Word.

John Quincy Adams many years ago showed a problem to the United States Senate. He showed the Senate two different bushels. A bushel is a basket-size used to measure farm crops. One bushel-size was from New York. The other was from South Carolina. One bushel was much bigger than the other. Later that same day he showed two different one-pound weights used for measuring. One was from Maine. The other was from Massachusetts. One pound weighed 13 ounces more than the other. He asked the senators how America could come together if bushels and pounds were different in some states. Everyone would be confused about the size of the bushel and the weight of a pound. It would be hard to buy and sell things between states. The government made a department called Bureau of Weights and Measures to stop that problem. A machine for weighing is in the Smithsonian Museum today. It has a circle around it. The machine is so careful when it weighs things that people must stand outside the circle. The machine will feel the heat from their bodies if people stand inside the circle. It will make the machine weigh wrong.

God has a way to weigh or measure us. His way to measure us is perfect. It is always right. The way God measures us is by His Word. God will not judge us by people's judgment. God is our critic. God will judge us by His Word.

God's Word: Clear in What It Says

The Bible is clear in what it says. Hebrews 4:2 (GNB) says, "We have heard the Good News, just as they did. They heard the message, but it did them no good, because when they heard it, they did not accept it with faith." The good news (gospel) is not hard to understand. It is not hard to know what is right and what is wrong. It is not hard to understand the biblical way of life. It is not hard to understand what it means to follow Jesus. The meaning in the Bible becomes hard to understand when a person's heart and mind are not wanting to understand. To understand the Bible is when people read the Bible with a heart that is open and full of faith.

Peter warned us to give attention to the Scripture. "It is like a lamp shining in a dark place" (2 Pet. 1:19, GNB). *Darkness* has the meaning of badness and not knowing. That kind of darkness is everywhere on this earth. The Word of God is the real truth. You and I can depend on it. The truth of God's Word shines into the lives and ways of all people on earth. It shines even in the darkest places.

Many Christians have heard the story of the Auca Indians. Some missionaries tried to take the good news about Jesus to the Auca Indians. Some Auca Indians killed the missionaries. Today, years later, many of the Auca Indians have become Christians. The light of God's Word has changed them from darkness to light. That is what God has done with His Word in all the world.

Some people say the Bible is not clear. They say it has a lot of things that do not agree (conflicts). That idea is really not right. We can see that God was making more and more things clear in the Bible. God was making Israel and the world ready for Jesus Christ. But the Bible must be seen as one whole book. The Bible is one book. Baptists believe all of the Scriptures. A person must read and study all the Bible. Then that person can understand what God wants to show us.

Paul told Timothy, "Do your best to win full approval in God's sight, as a workman who is not ashamed of his work, one who correctly teaches the message of God's truth" (2 Tim. 2:15, GNB). Second Peter 1:20 warns us. It says to be careful about having a private way to explain and understand the Bible. That is not handling the Word of Truth right. That is using the Bible to say what I want it to say.

A man worked with my father in business. He was not a Christian. That man had a heart attack. He was near death. I talked with that man about salvation. He later called me back into the room. He asked Jesus to be his Savior. His wife asked me to preach the funeral. That was what the man had wanted. She was a Jehovah's Witness. She asked me to read several Scriptures. I told her I would read the verses she wanted if they were from the Bible. She gave me a long list of verses. They were only parts of the verses. The clear meaning of the verses did not show up when only parts of verses were read. I read the whole verses when I preached the funeral. Satan uses Scriptures wrong by breaking up parts of verses and giving the wrong ideas. Parts of verses can change the real meaning of the verses. These parts can give people a wrong understanding.

The Bible shows that history has a meaning. To write the Bible took a long time. It took many hundreds of years. But the Bible still makes good sense by telling God's story. Some world religions think history is like a circle. They think history does the same things over and over again. Those religions see things happen like a nation becomes strong. Then that nation becomes weak, while some other nation becomes strong. They see the same things repeating. Those religions think people have the same repeated experience. They think people live many lives being born and then dying again and again. This is called reincarnation. Those religions believe that people can learn from what happens. They believe those people are stuck without any hope of real change within a lifetime. Christians see things differently. Christians do not see life as a circle. They see life as a line. Christians believe that history began one time in the past. Christians believe that history will end sometime in the future. Christians believe that things will end by God's plan. The Bible tells us these things.

The Bible talks about how God has shown Himself. The Bible talks about how God has shown what He wanted in His world. The Bible tells us that God has a goal for the world. We find when we study the Bible where God wants us in His plan. we find wonderful joy to be part of what God is doing. We become part of God's forever work. We see the Bible has one clear idea from God (message). All the different kinds of writing in the Bible have the same message from God.

Dr. B. H. Carroll was the dean of the Bible Department at Baylor University. He later became the first president of Southwestern Baptist Theological Seminary. Dr. Carroll, when he was a young man, thought he had found many places in the Bible that did not agree with other places in the Bible (contradictions). He studied the Bible closely. He found there were no places in the Bible that really did not agree with other places in the Bible (no contradictions). He had been able to understand every contradiction except for six. He said he was disposed to think that if he had more sense he could harmonize those other six.

The Word of God agrees through the whole Bible. It does not break up or show no agreement. The Word of God is filled with true facts. The Word of God has a clear single understanding of God.

God's Word: the Believer's Authority

Some people think the Bible is not clear enough. They think people cannot understand what the Bible teaches. Some people make strict lists of things that everyone must believe. A strict list of things everyone must believe is called a creed. John Leland was a Baptist pastor in America. Leland helped make sure that the American Constitution promised religious freedom. Leland warned against making creeds. He said creeds lead people to believe the creed more than God. He said creeds really keep people away from God. He said Baptists must only have one strict thing to believe—the Word of God. That advice was good for all time. Truth and freedom are in the Word of God. Baptist people in the past believed that. They worked hard to make sure that everyone can go to the Word of God and read it. He could understand it for himself. Baptist people in the past made it clear that no one must have a teacher or a priest to teach them the Word of God. Teachers are good. But, only the Holy Spirit can make the Word of God come alive.

John Wesley was a great preacher in the past. He started the Methodists. He won many people to Jesus. He was wise.

A person who writes songs had almost the same thought about the Bible. He wrote:

O Word of God Incarnate, O Wisdom from on high,
O Truth unchanged, unchanging, O Light of our dark sky:
We praise thee for the radiance That from the hallowed page,
A lantern to our footsteps, Shines on from age to age.
—William W. How

The Bible is God's Book. It is from God. It has full authority. It does not make mistakes. It does not have errors in it. It is given by God (God-breathed). It is fully true with no part a mistake.

PERSONAL LEARNING ACTIVITY 1

Match the Bible verses or portions of verses with the correct references.

Bible Verses

1. _____ Heaven and earth will pass away, but my words will never pass away.

2. _____ What gives life is God's Spirit; man's power is of no use at all. The words I have spoken to you bring God's life-giving Spirit.

3. _____ All Scripture is inspired by God and is useful for teaching the truth, rebuking error, correcting faults, and giving instruction for right living,

4. _____ For no prophetic message ever came just from the will of man, but men were under the control of the Holy Spirit as they spoke the message that came from God.

5. _____ You will know the truth, and the truth will set you free.

References

a. 2 Timothy 3:16
b. 2 Peter 1:21
c. John 8:32
d. John 6:63
e. Matthew 24:35

Answers: 1. e, 2. d, 3. a, 4. b, 5. c

CHAPTER 2

The Doctrine of God

God said [to Moses], "I am who I am."
Exodus 3:14 (GNB)

ONE OF THE RELIGIONS IN THE WORLD IS ISLAM. People who belong to that religion are called Moslems. The Moslems went to war more than 700 years after Jesus lived on earth. They won much of the land in the Middle and Near East. The Moslems tried to destroy all people who did not believe in God. Jews believe in one God. The Moslems permitted the Jews to keep their religion. The Moslems thought anyone who believed in more than one God believed a false religion. The Moslems tried to get others to join the Islam religion. The Moslems killed those people who would not join the Islam religion. The Moslems thought Christians believed in three Gods. The Moslems could not understand about the Christian belief in the Trinity. The Moslems thought the Trinity meant Christians believed in three Gods.

The Trinity: a Definition
The word *Trinity* is not in the Bible. Christians believe in the Trinity. That is a way to understand what the Bible teaches about God. The Bible shows that God is Father, Son, and Holy Spirit. The word *Trinity* is a word that explains what the Bible shows about God.

To explain the idea of Trinity is hard. For Christians to understand this idea is hard. Only God can fully understand Trinity. Christians believe it. The Bible teaches it. Christians believe it even if it is hard to understand.

The Old Testament showed God to us. We think about God in the Old Testament when we think about God the Father. Jesus prayed to God the Father. We sometimes talk about what God is like. We are talking about God the Father when we talk about what God is like. We are thinking about God the Father when we say the word *God.*

Some people may be surprised to find that it is the New Testament that talks about God the Father the most. The Old Testament does not talk much about God as Father. The New Testament talks a lot about God as Father. God is talked about as Father in the Old Testament when He is the Father of Israel. The Old Testament does not talk about one person knowing God as Father.

We find a different thing when we look in the New Testament. There are more than 170 times that God is called Father in the books of Matthew, Mark, Luke, and John (the Gospels). Jesus talks about God as His own Father. People who believe in God many times call Him Father. One good example is in the Model Prayer Jesus prayed. The idea of the Trinity is more clear in the New Testament than in the Old Testament. But all three—Father, Son, and Holy Spirit—are in the Old Testament, too.

Check your Bible to see the Holy Spirit and Jesus in the Old Testament. Genesis 1:2 (GNB) refers to the work of the Holy Spirit. That verse says, "The power of God was moving over the water." We can see the Son in many verses about the Messiah. The New Testament refers to Jesus (Logos) as the Creator of the world. (See John 1:3.) We can see all three—Father, Son, and Holy Spirit—have always been. All three were there when the world was made.

Here are some important verses that talk about all three Persons of the Trinity: Matthew 3:13-17; Romans 8:9; and Ephesians 1:17. Many other verses are about two Persons of the Trinity: Matthew 18:19-20; John 14:16; Acts 5:3-4; Romans 9:5; 1 Corinthians 12:3; 2 Corinthians 3:17-18; Ephesians 1:3. Christians started believing in the idea of Trinity because the Bible showed it clearly. Somehow, Christian belief must try to understand the facts of the Bible—all three (Father, Son, and Holy Spirit) are called God.

The Trinity: Some Wrong Ideas About Trinity

Christians have always tried to understand the idea of Trinity. People sometimes have tried to explain the Trinity. Some ways to explain the Trinity have been wrong. We can look at some of the wrong ways. That will help us know the right way to understand the Trinity.

The first wrong idea is that God showed Himself in different ways through history. Some people think God showed Himself as Father in the Old Testament. Then, He was Son in the New Testament. Then, He was Holy Spirit after Jesus went to heaven. This is not a right way to understand the Trinity. To explain the Trinity this way changes the idea of God always being Father, Son, and Holy Spirit. It explains God as being each of these for a short time. This idea is sometimes called *modalism.* The word *modalism* means that God appeared in different ways (different modes) at different times in the past.

The second wrong idea is that the Trinity is really three different Gods. This idea is called *tritheism.* The word *tritheism* means three Gods. This way to explain the Trinity really sees the Trinity as three Gods who are all equal. This way to explain the Trinity thinks that the three Gods work together. They plan together when they need to.

The third wrong idea is that Jesus became part of God some time in His life. This way to explain the Trinity says Jesus was just a normal human person. It says God the Father adopted Jesus. People who believe this idea think most of the time that Jesus was adopted by the Father when Jesus was baptized. These people think Jesus became part of God when He was baptized. This idea is called *adoptionism.* That word means that Jesus was adopted by God the Father. This idea thinks the Holy Spirit came to Jesus when Jesus was baptized. He made Jesus part of God.

None of these ideas match the Bible. Only one belief (doctrine) can match the Bible. This belief is that God is one. We can know God. God has shown Himself to us. God has shown Himself in three Persons. All three of those Persons are eternal. All three Persons have always been alive. The Father, Son, and Spirit are just one God. This idea cannot be fully understood by people. And there is no perfect word to use to make this idea clear.

We use the word *Person*. Sometimes that word makes us confused. That seems to be the best word to use. No one has found a better word. We say God in three Persons. That is the best way we can find to say the idea right.

We say that Father, Son, and Holy Spirit are all one Person. We are making it clear that God as Father, Son, and Holy Spirit has personality and inner nature. We cannot go on to think that the three Persons make God something more than one Person. Christians believe in only one God. To understand this idea of Trinity is hard. We Christians accept it as God's way to show Himself to us.

The One God: God's Spirit

Who is God? What is God like? Well, God is Spirit. There is no limit on God. God is fully perfect. God is a Person. God made all the world. God also takes care of the world now. God does things now in the world and in people's lives. God is leading the world in the way God planned.

The words above tell about God. (1) God is Person. (2) He is Spirit with no limits. He is perfect. (3) He is Creator. (4) He takes care of the world now. (5) He is working with His world now. (6) He is leading the world in the way God planned. We will see God as Father, Son, and Holy Spirit (Trinity) is doing all these things.

The words above explain about God. They say God is Spirit. Jesus told the woman at the well, "God is Spirit, and only by the power of his Spirit can people worship him as he really is" (John 4:24, GNB). The Second Commandment in the list of Ten Commandments means that God is Spirit. The Second Commandment says, "Do not make for yourselves images of anything in heaven or on earth or in the waters under the earth" (Ex. 20:4, GNB).

Baptists and many Protestants have always said that things like saints, statues, or other things do not help a person think about God. They really give the person a wrong idea about God. God is too great to be shown in a picture or a statue or something else. The only way a person can really see about God is to see what Jesus is. Jesus is God in human body. Pictures and statues cannot show Jesus to us.

A picture and a statue can be good art. But, they are not right for worship. God is spirit. He is so great that He cannot be made into a picture or a statue. God is in time, but He is greater than time. God is in the world that He made. But, God is greater than the world He made. God is involved in history. But, he is so much greater than history.

We see verses many times in the Old Testament that talk about God with human words. Wise people who study the Bible a lot call this *anthropomorphic* talking. That means to talk about God by using human words to try to explain what God is like. To find examples of this anthropomorphic talking is easy. The Bible, for example, talks about God's finger (Ex. 31:18), His footstool (1 Chron. 28:2), His arm (Num. 11:23), His face (Num. 6:25), His eyes (2 Chron. 16:9), and His hand (Ps. 37:24). The Bible is talking in the language that poets use when they talk like that. The Bible does not really mean that God has a physical human body as we do. The Bible is clear that God is spirit.

The One God: God Is Person

We talked about God as Person when we talked about Trinity. There are a few more things that need to be clear when we talk about God as Person. The Bible shows God as a Person. The Bible talks about God doing things the way a Person would do things. Here are some examples of things in the Bible that show God as a Person.

1. The Bible shows that God knows about Himself.

2. The Bible shows that God thinks and feels and makes decisions.

3. The Bible shows that God is free.

He deals with people (relates) in ways as a Person. God does things in the world. All these things are things that persons do. These are not things that an idea can do. The Bible says God made people in God's own image. We are persons as God is Person. God is not only an idea. He is a real Person.

The Bible has many different words that are names for God. *Elohim* is a Hebrew language word. That is the word Hebrew people used to mean God. That word is used many times in the

Old Testament to refer to God. It is the word used in Genesis 1:1. It means about the same as the English language word *god.* There are other words in the Old Testament that are used to refer to God. Here is a list of Hebrew language words that the Bible uses to refer to God: *El Shaddai, El Elyon, El Olam,* and *El Roi:*

1. *El Shaddai* means God Almighty.
2. *El Elyon* means most high God.
3. *El Olam* means everlasting God.
4. *El Roi* means God who sees me.

Also, the word *Lord* was used many times in the Old Testament and the New Testament to mean God.

God gave the Hebrew people one special word to use for God's name. That word is *Yahweh. Yahweh* means I Am. This is the name God told to Moses. This name tells us a lot about God. The name *Yahweh* comes from the Hebrew language word that means to be. Wise people who study the Bible a lot have tried to understand exactly what God meant in Exodus 3:14 when God said, "I am who I am." God meant many things when He said that to Moses. We know God meant He is the God who really lives. He always will live. God is also the one who made everything that is. The name *Yahweh* means all those things.

The One God: God Has No Limits (Infinite)

God has no limits. There are several ways to explain this idea. We will discuss five words that will help us understand that God has no limits (God is infinite). The five words that we will study are *eternal, immutable, omnipresent, omniscient,* and *omnipotent.*

God is eternal.—God did not have any beginning. God has no end. This means God is eternal. There has never been a time when God was not alive. People are limited. People live in a world of time. That makes it hard for people to understand how God is eternal. God is greater than time. God was already before the world began. God did not begin. He was not made by someone else. God will never stop. God's living has no limit.

God is immutable.—God does not change. God is, as the Bible says, the same yesterday, tomorrow, and forever (see Ps. 102:27; Heb. 13:8). This idea is hard for some people. The Bible says things like God "repented." About 13 times the Old Testament shows God changing His mind. (See Ex. 32:14; Deut. 9:19; 1 Sam. 15:11; 2 Sam. 24:16; 1 Kings 21:29; 1 Chron. 21:15; Ps. 106:45; Jer. 18:8; 26:3,19; Amos 7:3,6; Jonah 3:10.) All of these verses show God changing what He did. God changed what He did when people changed what they did. God never changed His goal. He never did something wrong against His own holy life. He never did things in a bad way. God promises to judge people when they sin. We can know that if people change away from sin that God will hold back His promised judgment. God does not change His character. God will always save when He promises to save people from sin. God does not change. He will punish sin. God does not change. He will lead the world in the way he plans. God's nature does not change.

God is omnipresent.—This word means that God is everywhere in the whole world all the time. God is always everywhere. The person who wrote Psalm 139 said: "Where can I go from your Spirit? Where can I flee [run away] from your presence? If I go up to the heavens, you are there; if I make my bed in the depths, you are there. If I rise on the wings of the dawn, if I settle on the far side of the sea, even there your hand will guide me, your right hand will hold me fast [strong]" (Ps. 139:7-10). This is a wonderful truth about God.

No one can get away from God at any time. Some people want to run away from God. This verse is a warning. No one can run away from God. This verse is also a promise for people who want God's help. God is always with us.

The prophet Elijah in the Old Testament made fun of the prophets who worshiped Baal. Baal was a god made of stone. Elijah said that maybe Baal had gone away on a trip. Baal could not hear the prayers of the people who worshiped him. Elijah's God was never gone away. Elijah's God was always with Elijah. And God is always with all believers everywhere in the world at the same time.

God is omniscient.—This word means that God knows all things. God knows everything. God understands every person everywhere at the same time. God knows what is inside our hearts. God also knows everything about science. Some people think they really know a lot. People have learned much about the world because of science. Now some people think they do not need God. They think they know so much. Those people should compare what they know to what God knows. God knows more than everyone. This is the truth. People who believe in God should give their lives fully to God. God knows us better than we know ourselves. God knows us well. His will for our lives is best. We should give our lives to God. (See Rom. 12:2.)

God is omnipotent.—That word means that God has all power. Nothing in all the world has more power than God. The Bible teaches that God has *all* power. Satan might have a little power. Bad government leaders might have a little power. They have a little power only because God lets them have a little power. We must remember what Jesus said to the disciples. The disciples watched Jesus go up to the Father. Jesus' body was gone. The disciples were going to face a world that was angry. This world did not believe. It would hurt them. It was mixed up. This world was hungry for power.

The Roman armies seemed strong—with their soldiers' clothes and their war boots. The disciples remembered that Jesus said, "I have been given all authority in heaven and on earth" (Matt. 28:18, GNB). Some day, the Bible says, God's trumpet will make its loud noise. Loud voices will shout from heaven and say: You need to be in God's group if you want to be with the group that has real power and will win. You need to be a follower of Jesus (disciple).

The One God: God Is Perfect

We said in the words above that God is *perfect Spirit.* Those two words fit together. God is spirit. God has no limits. Nothing can stop God. We say that God is *perfect.* We say that God has no limits *(infinite).* Those two words fit together. Those two words tell us a lot about God Himself. We will use these two words to help us think about what God is like. We will think about God's character. God's character means to think about what God is like. Four words can help us think about what God is like—His character. The four words are *holiness, righteousness, truth,* and *love.*

Sometimes when we use the word *holy* we get a wrong idea

about what it means. Sometimes we think a holy (set apart, different) person is someone who wears old clothes or does not use any makeup. Maybe we think holy things are the things in a church. These ideas are not the full idea of holiness that the Bible shows us. Some wise people who study the Old Testament a lot say that we must understand that God is holy. They say we cannot understand the Old Testament if we do not understand that God is holy. The word *holy* is used some different ways in the Bible. The Bible uses the word *holy* in about three ways:

1. Holy can mean God's way.
2. Holy can mean some things that are used only for God.
3. Holy can mean to live in some good ways.

God's way is fully holy. His way is different from the way of the world. The priests worked only for God in Old Testament times. They were a special group for God's work. They were holy. The priests used special things in the Temple for worship. These special Temple things could not be used for everyday life. They could only be used for worship. That made those special Temple things holy. People do things God's way when people are holy. People live a life that is used for God when they are holy.

Leviticus 19:1 (GNB) says, "Be holy, because I, the Lord your God, am holy." This command was written after some rules about worship and living with other people and sins. That helps us understand that we should live in a good way that shows we belong to a good God. Our thoughts should be used for God. Our lives should be given fully to God. The way we live should be the good way God wants us to live. We can see God is fully holy in everything.

God is righteous. Righteousness is part of what God is like— His character. We mean that God always is right and He always is against wrong when we say God is righteous. Everything God does is right. God also has told us what is right and what is wrong. God's Word tells us what is right and what is wrong. God can judge against all wrong because He is righteous. God can punish us when we do what is wrong because He is righteous. Jesus died on the cross. He gave His blood for us. The righteous God is ready to forgive people who are not righteous (sinners).

All of us are sinners. We are not righteous. But the righteous God still works to give life to all people who are not righteous.

God is full of truth. Everything that is true comes from God. Nothing about God is untrue. God is always true. His truth will never change. People cannot know the full truth without knowing God. People can learn some true things. No person without God can understand all those true things in the right way. Everything that is true comes from God. Things that are true about science, philosophy, and religion also come from God. Something that is true is always true. People sometimes think the truth of science shows that God is not true. The person who believes God and who wants to know more about the world will see that the truth of God is the greatest of all true things. The truth of God is not different from real true things in science.

God is love. God's love is the kind of love that wants people to have the best possible life. God loves us like that. It cost God a lot to love like that. A beautiful story about Hosea and Gomer is in the Old Testament. Gomer was not a faithful wife. But Hosea loved her so much that he never stopped loving her. This is a picture of what God's love is like. People are sinners against God. God still loves people. A story in the New Testament is about a prodigal (wasteful) son. This story is about a father's great love for his son. The son was bad to his father. The father loved him anyway. This pictures God's love. Jesus showed clearly God's love for people when Jesus died on the cross. God's love is full of mercy and grace. Sinners would be doomed without His love.

The One God: God Is Creator

God is creator. This means God made everything. We really mean more than that God just made everything when we say God is Creator. We also mean when we say God is Creator that God made everything. Now He takes care of everything He made. God is still working with what He made. God is leading everything He made. Everything God made will end the way God planned in the future.

God is Creator of all.—God made all things. People should be able to learn about God by looking at what He made. People usually do not find God when they study what God made. Romans 1 tells us God has shown Himself in what He has made. People should be able to find God by seeing what He made. People do not have an excuse for not knowing God. God shows Himself in the world He made.

People build idols when they look for God in the things God has made. Some people try to find out the future by reading the stars (astrological charts). Some people worship the sun and moon. Some people have wild parties for the changes in the seasons. People often worship the things God made instead of God when they study the world God made. Many people start to believe that there is no God. These people have no excuse before God for their mistake. We cannot understand God by looking at what God made and then moving back to understand the God who made all things. The right way is for us to study about God first. We then will be able to understand about what God made (creation). We study God to learn more about His creation. We do not study creation so we can find God. All that God made does make us feel really good (inspired). We see His world. We want to praise Him. This is right for us to do. We also must think and ask some questions when we see what God has made. We need to ask:

1. Why did God make the whole world?
2. Why did God make people in His own image?
3. Why did God make people free?
4. What does God plan for the world He made?
5. How is God still working with His world?

These are some of the questions we need to think about.

God is separate from His creation.—To understand creation (all that God made), we need to see that God is separate from what He made. Some people are called pantheists. These people believe God lives in all things. These people believe a little bit of God is in each tree, each cloud, each mountain and valley, each stream, and each flower. The Bible teaches that God is separate from what He made. The world is not God. It is not part of God. God does not need the things He created to help Him live.

God had a reason to create.—God created all things for a reason. Why did God make the whole world if He did not need it? A black poet named James Weldon Johnson wrote a poem with God saying, "I'm lonely." These simple words are almost right. We cannot think God was lonely. We cannot think God needed to create people to make Him feel better. We can understand better why God created everything when we understand two things about God. We need to understand about God's love and His glory. A parent does not need a child. Parents' lives feel richer when they have a loving child. We say God does not need all the world He has made. God is enriched by all His creation. Wise people study the Bible for many years. Protestants generally have said God made the world for His glory. That is true. That is part of God's reason for making the whole world. But God's love helps us understand God's glory. God gets the glory when the people He made happily give glory to Him. People in the future will give God the full glory that is really His. This glory is shown in the Bible in the Book of Revelation.

Revelation shows everyone giving glory to God in the new heaven and the new earth. People become fully happy and satisfied when they give glory to God. The Book of Revelation shows heaven and the people in heaven full of joy. God made everything because of His love for us. God is most pleased when we are fully loving Him. We can then see how God made the world for His own glory when we understand that. This understanding of God should support all of our thoughts about God. It should support all of our lives, too.

God did not use anything to make all the world. He created out of nothing *(ex nihilo)*. Christians sometimes talk a lot about how God made everything. It is important to understand that God made everything out of nothing. He did not use anything when He made everything. We would have to back up and explain where the things God used came from if God used something to make everything. The Bible is clear. It says God spoke and everything in the whole world (universe) began. Speaking was all God needed to do. Nothing would have been made if God had not spoken.

God sustains His creation.—Colossians 1:17 (NLV) talks about Christ Jesus. That verse says, "Christ was before all things. All things are held together by Him." Nehemiah 9:6 talks about

God making everything and how wonderful God is. That verse says, "And thou preservest [take care of] them all" (KJV). Many other verses in the Bible say that the world continues only because God still takes care of the world. We say God takes care of (sustains) the world. We also mean:

1. The power that moves the whole world comes from God.
2. God is always working in His world He made.
3. Everything God made is still under His control.
4. God did not make the whole world and then leave it alone to take care of itself.

God takes care of His world. He sustains it. God made the whole world to follow rules. We can call these rules the natural process. God made the rules for the world. God cooperates with the natural process He made. Here are two ideas that must be avoided: (1) God never touches the natural laws He made. (2) God never uses the natural laws He made when He does something in the world. No. 1 means that God is in control of the world He made. God can suspend a natural law and do a miracle when He wants to. Some people do not believe God does miracles. That does not change God's power to do whatever He wants to do. God still controls what He made. The world is not out of God's hands now. No. 2 means God is careful with the natural laws He made. God often uses the natural laws of the world to do what He wants. This does not deny miracles. Exodus 14:21 (NLV) clearly shows that God used "a strong east wind" to turn back the waters. This is an example of how God uses the natural laws He made.

God takes care of His world. He is still involved with what He made. People who believe in God see that this is wise thinking. Here is the way believers think about this.

1. Everything in the whole world is here because God made it.
2. God only made the world because He had a good reason to make the whole world.
3. God will stay involved with the world He made to make sure His reasons are fulfilled.

We must look at all of history to see God's work in history. God is involved in history in any way He wants to be involved.

He may change history the way He wants. He may change the way things normally happen. He may change what happens in a battle or in a war or in government. He may change the things a person does. He can have a special relationship with a believer. These are hard things to understand. A lot of books could be written about these ideas. "God is involved in His creation" is a wonderful true thing.

God moves His world in the ways He wants. This idea is called Providence. Providence involves ideas like God knowing things before they happen. Many Christians, including Baptists, used to argue about this idea. The argument was between predestination and free will. God planned what would happen in the world before He made it. God knew all the things that would happen in the world before He made the world. This helps us understand these two true things: (1) The hope Christians have is based on this sure thing. God will defeat everything that is against Him. He will bring the world to the end He has planned. (2) Every believer has a place in working with God in His great plan.

The One God: God Is Sovereign

In the book *The Axioms of Religion*, E. Y. Mullins says the basic theological truth (axiom) is "The holy and loving God has a right to be sovereign." *Sovereign* means above all others or supreme. Mullins talks in the chapter on the theological axiom about the way God shows His sovereignty in His workings with the world and with the people He made. God's sovereignty makes the basis for the priesthood of believers.

We mean that God is in control when we say He is sovereign. We must understand God's sovereignty if we want to understand God and people. We do not have to believe in real strong predestination when we believe God is sovereign. Some people who believed in real strong predestination sometimes did not talk much about the priesthood of believers.

Southern Baptists have always been concerned that lost people become saved. We have been evangelistic. We have not usually been people who believed in real strong predestination. Often people who believe in real strong predestination have not been evangelistic. This should show that belief in God's sovereignty does not mean that a person must start to believe in real strong predestination. The belief in the priesthood of believers really comes from the idea of the sovereignty of God. The belief in the priesthood of believers says that God does not give away His sovereignty to any other person or organization. God always relates straight with each person.

We do not mind the idea that God is sovereign when we understand that God is holy and loving. The truth is that we want a God like that to lead our lives. One question we think about is, Why doesn't God just make this world like He wants it if He is sovereign and controls all things? We can find the answer to that question when we understand that God made people to be free. God does not break our freedom. He does not want to break His reason for making people.

God's sovereignty touches everything in the whole world. He is sovereign over what He made. He is sovereign over every person. He is sovereign over every power. All power that is in the world is here because God permits it. He is sovereign over the believer. God means for the believer to accept His control with loving obedience.

God Shows Himself as Father
We already saw that the idea of God as Father is mostly a New Testament idea. People thought about God as cold and strict when Jesus came. Hebrew people thought God was so far away and so holy that they would not even say God's name. A Hebrew person passed over God's name in silence when he was reading the Bible and came to God's name. God later was called "the name." Jesus did things differently from that. Jesus taught His children to pray, "Our Father." Jesus taught a new relationship. God is Father. We are His children. This new relationship became part of the good news Christians preached. Christians used the word *Abba* as Jesus had used it (Rom. 8:15; Gal. 4:6). *Father* is not really the right way to translate the Aramaic word *Abba*. The word *Abba* is a family word that means something like *daddy*. We cannot be careless about our relationship with God. God is not the "man upstairs." But we are free to "approach God's throne, where there is grace" with confidence (Heb. 4:16,

GNB).

God Shows Himself as Son
We do not mean that God made Jesus at any point in time when we say Jesus is God's Son. Jesus has always been alive. He is God. There is no God apart from Jesus and no Jesus apart from God.

God Shows Himself as Holy Spirit
The Holy Spirit is first talked about in the Bible in Genesis 1:2 (NLV): "The Spirit of God was moving over the top of the waters." The Spirit is the third person of the Godhead. The Spirit is eternal like the first and second person. The Spirit is talked about sometimes in the Old Testament. The Bible in the last part of the Old Testament talks about when the Spirit would come in great power. The Spirit was involved in Jesus' birth. The Spirit was with Jesus during His ministry. The Day of Pentecost was the day the Old Testament was fulfilled and the Holy Spirit came in His fullness.

PERSONAL LEARNING ACTIVITY 3

Imagine that a non-Christian friend asked you to explain how a Christian can believe in one God but still believe in the Trinity. Write how you would explain in the lines below.

CHAPTER 3

In God's Image

Then God said, "And now we will make human beings; they will be like us and resemble us. They will have power over the fish, the birds, and over all animals, domestic and wild, large and small." Genesis 1:26 (GNB)

Many people long ago believed man was the greatest thing God made. For people to believe that was easy. Now scientists have found many new things about how big the whole world (universe) is.

In God's Image: Man, the Goal of Creation

We already learned when we studied about God that we do not study what God has made and then try to understand God from what He made. God shows (reveals) Himself. People are limited. We cannot know God unless God shows (reveals) Himself to us . Our ideas about God, His world, His purpose, and what people are like should follow and depend on what God shows us. Our ideas about ourselves should not be our guide.

The Bible shows humans are the greatest thing God made. Humans were always the goal of what God made. We do not become proud when we hear that. That should make us humble. That should make us want to worship God with great thanks. Our deep feelings should lead us to give real praise to God when we look out into space. He made all of it for us. Is there life on other planets? We do not know. There is much we do not know. Things we do not know do not bother the faith of believers. Anything else that lives in space does not change what God is like. It does not change the truth God has showed us about people. It does not change salvation.

In God's Image: Persons, like God

We talked in chapter 2 about what *personhood* means. We find when we compare God to people or people to God that we have some of the same characteristics as God. This is true even though God has no limits and humans are limited. God is spirit. (See John 4:24.) Humans are physical and spiritual. (See Gen. 2:7.) These things show differences between God and man. God and humans, however, share personhood.

Both men and women were made in God's image. Many people in the Middle Ages thought God made man in His image. They thought God then made woman out of man's image. This idea is not in the Bible. Genesis 1:27 (GNB) says, "God created human beings, making them to be like himself. He created them male and female." The Hebrew word for *man* is *adam*. *Adam*, in Hebrew, means mankind, including both men and women. God made all people in His own image. Both male and female show God's image.

God made people in His image. God gave people the wonderful gift of personhood. We are like God in many ways. People have intelligence. They can think about hard things. Animals do not have these same abilities, like humans. We are able to think about our own selves. We are able to think about other people and new ideas. We can make decisions about the way we live. Animals only have instincts. Our ability to make decisions about love makes it possible for us to choose to give love, no matter what happens or how people react to our love. We have free will. Free will is the right to choose from many different choices. *Free will* means we have the right to choose what is right or choose what is wrong. We also have an inner feeling of right and wrong. This is called a conscience. Our conscience is not always a perfect guide to do what is right or wrong. A conscience is a characteristic only people have.

In God's Image: Persons Are a Unity

People are both spiritual and physical. That does not split people up into two or even three different parts. A person is just one being. A person is not split up. One person is made of a body and soul—or body, soul, and spirit. That person is not a soul that lives in a body. That idea of a soul that lives in a body is called a *dichotomy.*

The Greek people had an idea the soul was a separate thing from the body. They thought the body was just a house the soul lived in. This idea still comes up sometimes. Some people who have this idea think the body can do whatever it wants to. They think what happens to the body does not do anything to the soul. This idea comes from Greek ideas from long before Jesus was born.

Men such as Plato and Aristotle, Greek philosophers who lived long before Jesus was born, believed the soul or reason (sometimes they would use the word *reason* instead of the word *soul*) was just like God. Those people thought the body was material. It was therefore bad. They thought such as this: If the body is bad, then it will live in bad ways. The soul is much better than the body. It is like God. It is not touched by the bad body.

An idea called "gnosticism" began after Jesus lived. Gnosticism believed many things like the Greek ideas we talked about above. Many New Testament writers wrote against the ideas of gnosticism. Monasticism was when people started living in monasteries or living by themselves. They were living hard lives. They thought that would make God happy. One reason why monasticism began was because of these ideas of good souls and bad bodies.

Yes, it is true that a person's body has a big influence on the way a person thinks about himself. A person's body influences the way a person gets along with other people. A person who is small must learn ways to make up for having less strength than a large, strong person. A good-looking man or a beautiful woman will learn how to get along with people in different ways than a person who is not good looking. Some people might say this would not be true in a perfect world. But the idea here is that the body and the mind cannot be separated. The soul cannot be separated from the body. It is true that the earthly body will be left at death. Paul said we will have a heavenly body (1 Cor. 15:35-44).

In God's Image: Persons Are Related

We read the story in Genesis about God making the world. We see all people of the earth have come from the same parents. Our first parents were made in the image of God. Any belief that says one race of people is better than some other race of people does not agree with the clear teaching of Scripture. All people are made in the image of God. We need to understand this truth. All people are related to one another. Now we can really start to see our responsibility for telling the good news about Jesus (evangelism) and missions. We can help people in need. We can try to make peace in our world. We can do other things that make better relationships between people.

In God's Image: Persons Have Potential

We say persons have potential. That means people have the inner possibility to do some good things. We know when we look at all people together as a group that all people together have the potential to do some good things. God told the man and the woman to fill the earth when He made them. God told them to take charge of it. God told them to rule over all the animals in it (Gen. 1:28). People have made progress in the world. That is because people are slowly doing those things God told the first people to do.

The word *ecology* means the careful balance of all nature. Some people said when the ecology movement first started that Christians used Genesis 1:28 as an excuse to ruin the ecology. This was not true. Christians became aware of the careful balance in nature as soon as other people. Christians started to say that taking charge of the earth meant to use it in good and careful ways for the good of all people. People who believe God made all things have great respect and reverence for the careful balance of nature (ecology). Christian people help the things ecology is concerned about.

Each person also has the ability for good. Walter Thomas Conner wrote the book *Revelation and God* (Broadman Press, 1936). Conner said, "The incarnation shows man's capacity for God" (p. 53). Conner meant that when God became a man in Jesus, each person has a place in his life for God. Jesus showed the world how God wants each person to live his life. Sometimes the word *perfect* in the Bible means complete or mature. We must, however, see that God still expects us to live in a perfect way. We have sinful natures that keep us from living in a perfect way (Rom. 7). This does not make God's requirement for perfect living any less. There are many verses in the Bible that call for perfect living. One is "Be holy, because I, the Lord your God, am holy" (Lev. 19:1, GNB) and the clear command, "You must be perfect—just as your Father in heaven is perfect" (Matt. 5:48, GNB). This verse does not mean, "Be mature as your heavenly Father is mature." We cannot reach the goal to be perfect. (No one can live in sinless perfection.) That is the goal we are to work toward.

Look at Jesus' life and see the right picture of a person living the way God wanted. The Holy Spirit gives the power and the leadership to live right. Each person has great possibility (potential). Christians for many centuries have believed people sin by nature. Christians believe people will usually sin when they have opportunity. Some people in the past few years have said Christians have a low view of human nature. This is both true and false.

Christians have a low view of a person's ability to be good (potential) when that person does not know Christ. All of history, even in the last few years, shows that Christians are right. Christians have a high view of people who have been saved. Some religions say people can become like God—or even become a god. Even these religions do not have as high a hope for people as the New Testament gives to saved people. No religion is equal to Christianity in the way Christianity gives great potential to life before death.

God promised Christians He will guide each willing person to reach the highest good in life. God promises the highest good to Christians in relationships with other people. God promises the highest good to Christians in living right and in making good decisions. He promises the highest good to Christians in living wise, in doing good work, and in helping the world around us. God also promises the highest good in feeling fulfilled inside and in the joy of life.

God made people to be born again. A person, born as a baby, needs nine months before it is born. A terrible thing happens when the baby is not born. Many people live all through this life and never know the new birth. They never become what God made them to be. People are physically born to be born again (born of God).

God see things differently from the way most people see things. The world thinks some things are wonderful that God see as worthless. A person is ready to throw away many worthless things when he meets Jesus in salvation. Paul found the really important things in Jesus. Paul threw his old sense of important things in the trash. Paul got rid of his old ideas as a butterfly gets rid of its old cocoon. Paul was free in Christ.

Nietzsche was a German philosopher who did not like what it meant to become a Christian. He said that accepting Christ made a person give up the ancient values. He said all the great things— like power and being pushy and only depending on yourself— were ended by the cross. The cross gives a message about love, patience, humbleness, forgiveness, and grace. Thank God He was right. We become new people when we meet Jesus at the cross.

In God's Image: Persons Are Created Free

The doctrine of the priesthood of believers is talked about in chapter 7. Here we need to see that this doctrine also is true before a person is saved, meaning every person has freedom. The more freedom is stopped, the more people try without success to solve problems in the world. Some governments have forced religion on people. The governments have not given people freedom in matters of faith. People have an outer show of religion when this happens. They may not have a true faith in their hearts. God made people like himself. God is free. Baptists for 400 years have said that every person has the right to choose Christ or not to choose Him. There is in the American Constitution the line that says all men are created equal. That is the biblical idea about how God made people.

People will want to be a part of a group (community) of free people when they are free like this and they live the right way as free people. Each person sees that everyone is equal to the other people in the group (community). Free people together seek good for everyone when this happens. Freedom will help us minister to other people as servants when we understand freedom in the right way. Everyone living free will serve others. A person wants others to enjoy the freedom when he is truly and fully free in Jesus Christ. Free Christians will try to help other people become free in Christ. This helps us understand why many missionaries in the world today are sent by free churches.

Fallen in Sin: the Origin of Sin (Where Did Sin Come From?)

No one has been able to answer fully the problem of evil and suffering. The idea of gnosticism was accepted by some Christians early in Christian history. Gnosticism came from the Greek ideas that separated body and soul. This gnostic idea said that the evil came from the body. People who believed this idea said there is no more sin when the body is dead.

Some people think sin happens because people do not know any better. They think people are ignorant. People who believe this idea think education and good culture will someday end sin. This is a wrong idea, too. Other people say sin came from Satan. These people think sin was in the world before Adam and Eve sinned. The people who believe this idea use Jude 6; 2 Peter 2:4; and 1 John 3:8 to support their idea. These verses do show Satan as a bad sinner. Many wise people who study the Bible a lot think the verses do not say anything more than that Satan is a bad sinner.

A better idea is that sin is in the world because God made people free. Satan would have no way to do his evil work if people were not free. People used their freedom in the wrong way. This is why humanity fell into sin. People are free to decide to do right or wrong. Sin could not have started in the world without that freedom.

Fallen in Sin: the Results of Sin

Often we talk about "The Fall." We are talking about when Adam and Eve sinned. Adam and Eve were close to God. They were innocent. But they chose to disobey God. They fell from their innocence into sin.

The temptation Adam and Eve faced has been talked about in three different ways. They wanted something good God decided not to give them. They wanted something that looked beautiful. They wanted to get a new knowledge. Often temptation comes to us in these three ways.

No matter how you talk about Adam and Eve's temptation, the important thing to see is that Adam and Eve decided to do what God did not want. Frank Stagg wrote in *New Testament Theology* about Adam and Eve: "It is the story of man's self-love, self-trust, and self-assertion. First came the doubt of God: Is God's will really good for us? Are God's commands binding? Cannot one manage for himself? Doubt became distrust and then disobedience." (Broadman Press, 1962, p. 19).

We use the words *original sin*. These words are used for the doctrine that says all humans since Adam and Eve have been born into sin. David cried out, "I have been evil from the time I was born; from the day of my birth I have been sinful" (Ps. 51:5, GNB). This idea can be explained in several ways. Paul wrote, "Sin came into the world through one man, and his sin brought death with it. As a result, death has spread to the whole human race because everyone has sinned" (Rom. 5:12, GNB).

The doctrine of original sin is what gave people the idea to baptize babies. People who baptize babies think that as soon as possible after the baby is born the baby must be baptized. They believe that baptism washes away the child's sin. They believe the baby will go to hell if it dies if the child is not baptized. Some reformers in the time of the reformation changed their idea of infant baptism. They said infant baptism was the way children came into the Christian group (community) like circumcision in the Old Testament.

Baptists believe in original sin. But Baptists say no one goes to hell because he has inherited sin. Baptists believe each person becomes responsible for his own sin at the age of accountability. God does not judge a person's sin (hold a person accountable) until that person is old enough to know the difference between right and wrong. That age is different for each person.

We sometimes use the words *total depravity*. These words come from Calvinism. Many Baptists use these words. *Total depravity* means that each person is born ready to sin. This idea is connected to original sin, but this idea allows several different explanations for original sin. Some writers say that there is something passed from parents to children that make the children sin. This something may be spiritual or physical. These writers say that sin has been passed down from Adam to every person alive today. Other writers feel that the people in the world are evil. They believe that because all people in the world are evil everyone born in the world will become evil.

For us to know how sin is passed on in the world is not really important. Our question is if humans have a sinful nature that will make people sin or if humans must be punished because they are sinners by nature. This second idea says that in some way every person is judged guilty because of Adam's sin. Some people say that every person was somehow there with Adam. They say that every person was involved with Adam's sin and must be punished for that sin. This idea is called Federalism.

Total depravity is really easy to understand. It does not mean everyone born is as bad as he can become. It does not mean the sinner can do no good. It does not mean the sinner has no knowledge about God. People are basically going to do wrong rather than right. Today many people believe in Humanism. Humanism thinks the opposite of total depravity. Humanism thinks that people are basically good. They will do good if they have a chance to do so. Which of these two ideas a person has will influence how that person tries to change the world. Which of these two ideas a person has will influence how that person tries to evangelize the world.

Fallen in Sin: the Nature of Sin
Sin is everywhere. Many people who do not like the words *total depravity* still accept this truth that sin is everywhere (universal). Maybe these people are more against the words *total depravity* than they are against the idea. Really, the idea of total depravity and the idea that sin is everywhere are the same. The Bible clearly teaches that sin is everywhere. (See Ps. 14:1-3; 51:5; Jer. 17:9;

Luke 11:13; Rom. 3:9-18; Rom. 5:12-21; Eph. 2:3.)

The Bible talks clearly about the results of sin: "Sin pays its wages—death" (Rom. 6:23, GNB). This verse is talking about physical death and spiritual death. God told Adam and Eve they would die because of sin (Gen. 3:19). Sin made the people separated from God. Sin made shame and guilt. It made broken relationships with other people. Sin caused pain, suffering, and loss of freedom. Being stuck in sin and the death of the body are caused by sin.

David wrote Psalm 51. Psalm 51 is different from Psalm 23. Psalm 51 talks about deep, dark hurt feelings. How could one man write both of these psalms? The answer is because of sin.

Psalm 51 shows what sin does to a person. The psalm shows the pain David had after his sin with Bathsheba. David planned to kill Bathsheba's husband. Many bad things happened after all this sin. David was hurt by his own sins. David told Nathan, "I have sinned against the Lord" (2 Sam. 12:13, GNB). He took the full responsibility. He did not blame sin on his family before him. He did not blame his children. He did not blame the world around him. He did not blame the sense of right and wrong the people around him had. He did not blame Bathsheba or Uriah. He said it was his own sin. David let an awful sin come into his life. It robbed him of joy in God. Sin hurt his life. Sin hurt all his family and all his children. Sin ruined the lives of his children and grandchildren. David was a godly king. The people did not trust him as much as before he sinned. David's sin hurt the army. The army did not love David as much as before.

Sin makes the sinner dirty inside. David felt this burden so much he cried out (v. 7) for God to make him clean. David remembered what it was like to be clean. David wanted God to make him clean inside again. David said the dirt of sin was like having broken bones. It felt that bad. David did not have joy in his life. He felt depressed.

Sin can make a person feel bad in his body. Some people may remember a book from a few years ago called *Whatever Became of Sin?* That writer said things the world today does not want to hear. That book said sin can do things to a person's health. Paul talked about taking the Lord's Supper (1 Cor. 11). He warned that some people were taking the Lord's Supper with wrong feelings in their hearts. He said, "That is why many among you are weak and sick, and a number of you have fallen asleep [died]" (1 Cor. 11:30). This verse can mean several things. But this verse surely means that sin in a person's life hurts that person's health. The sin that hurts a person's body does not have to be sins such as alcohol, drugs, or tobacco. Any kind of sin can hurt our bodies.

David wanted a clean heart and a right spirit. David was proud. He tried to hide his sin. David was the king. He thought he could get away with murder and sex sin because he was the king. But David found that a bad punishment came on him when he used his power wrong. He cried out, "I am always conscious of my sins" (Ps. 51:3, GNB). He asked God to free his spirit (v. 12).

Sin separates the sinner from God. David prayed in verse 11 (GNB), "Do not banish [throw] me from your presence; do not take your holy spirit away from me."

Sin stops a person from telling other people about Jesus. David said when God forgave his sin, "Then I will teach sinners your commands, and they will turn back to you" (Ps. 51:13, GNB).

Our sin does things to God, too. Psalm 51 gets it starting idea from 2 Samuel 12:13. David said, "I have sinned against the Lord" (2 Sam. 12:13, GNB). He said it again in Psalm 51:4. David said he knew God would judge against his sin (v. 4). David thought like this: "Lord, if you do not punish me, if you do not do something about this sin and immorality in my life, people are going to say you're not a just judge. Lord, it's not only my reputation that is on the line, but yours as well."

Our sin does things to other people. David's sin was against Bathsheba. David lusted for her. David and Bathsheba's child had died. Uriah was sent to his death in war. David's son Absalom tried to take David's place as king. Another son Amnon raped his own half-sister. He was killed because of it. Who can know how much David's sin hurt the history of Israel? No one can doubt this. Sin hurts many people other than the one who sins. If a country wants to keep going, the people who live in it must live in right ways. Isaiah 3:8 (GNB) says: "Jerusalem is doomed! Judah is collapsing! Everything they say and do is against the Lord; they openly insult God himself."

It would be a good Bible study to follow each of David's children and see how David's sin hurt each one. The Old Testament teaches that a person's sin hurts his children and grandchildren and great grandchildren. Ezekiel said children could no longer blame their parents for their sins. Ezekiel saw the future gospel when each person would be responsible for his own sin. That is what the New Testament says about sin. Yes, each person is responsible for his own sin. But it is still true that the children and grandchildren are hurt when the parents sin. God does not judge children for their parents' sin. When parents fail, that does not give an excuse to the children to sin. God is merciful. We will, if we go on in our sin, start problems that will continue for our children and their children and on and on.

A man was watching birds on the Isle of Man years ago. He watched an eagle fly from the sky. It picked up a small animal. The eagle flew back into the sky. The eagle was a beautiful thing to see. The man watched with his binoculars. But the eagle started to fly in a strange way. Soon the eagle fell to the earth. The man thought the eagle was dead. He ran to where the eagle fell. He saw feathers everywhere. He soon found the eagle. He turned the eagle over. Then he knew what happened. The eagle picked up an animal called a badger. The eagle pulled the badger up to his chest. The badger ate at the eagle. It hit the eagle's heart. The eagle would not let the badger go, so the eagle died.

Sin is like that. We pick up sin. We hold it to ourselves. Sin destroys us. But we do not want to let it go.

A Description of Sin

There are several different words that tell what human sin is like. We can study these words. We can understand better about the problem man has living in sin.

Doing wrong. The Hebrew language word *aven* means iniquity. *Aven* has the idea of something twisted or crooked. It means a person's way of living is crooked and wrong. It means to be unholy, wrong, and against God's way of living. All sin is like this. Every sin breaks God's command, "Be holy, because I, the Lord your God, am holy" (Lev. 19:1, GNB).

Living in rebellion. Adam and Eve did this kind of sin. They knew what God told them about not eating the fruit. But they ate the fruit. They knew better. They disobeyed. This sin knows the law. It breaks the law. The English word *enmity* is this kind of sin. A person in this sin sets his mind against God or against some other person. Christ broke down the enmity between people by the cross. Christ broke down the enmity between people and God by the cross.

This sin is like rebellion. The words used to talk about this sin are a little different. This sin is like going across the borderline or not staying inside the lines when painting something. This is not going over the border made by people. It is going over the border made by God. This sin means to break the law because a person wanted to break the law.

Transgression. *Pasha* in the Hebrew language means to be like an outlaw, living in open rebellion. This sin is going against what God wants, against God's will. This sin is breaking the borders that God sets. I saw people like this during the years I worked for the Lord. Some people told me they will go the way they want to, no matter what the Bible says.

Missing the mark. This idea about sin comes from the Hebrew language word *chata*, which means to fall short of the goal or mark. God's law makes the target that our lives must aim at. We miss God's target when we sin. *Chata* can mean one sin or a way of life. A terrible thing is in a person's life when he lives outside God's plan.

Unbelief. People have an attitude of unbelief. They do not believe. The reason for all sin is unbelief. One work the Holy Spirit does is make the world feel guilty because the world does not believe in Christ (John 16:8-9).

Break the covenant. The word *covenant* means agreement. God made an agreement (covenant) with Israel. The covenant required Israel to live in a right way and to do God's work. God often punished Israel. Israel broke the agreement. Sin is doing wrong things. We are sinning when we do not do fully the work God has for us. We break the agreement with God when we do not fellowship with God. Jeremiah 31:34 talks about the new covenant. The new covenant is put in our hearts. We call God

"Father" under the new covenant. To have a relationship like that with God is wonderful. We are sinning when we forget about this wonderful relationship.

Ungodliness. The word means not to be reverent to God.

Debauchery. This word in the New Testament means to live only to please the feelings of the body.

Depravity. This word talks about the way a person is. Depravity is not only talking about what a person does. Depravity, like another Greek word, means to be bad and full of wickedness.

Sin against God. All the words in this list and some other words help us understand what sin is like. We must see that sin is doing things against God and against His will. Paul said this in Romans 1. Paul said that God showed Himself through all the things He made. But man still rebelled against what God showed to him. People went into bad sin. They kept on sinning. Many wise people who study about God think that all sins comes from selfish feelings in people. People want more for themselves. People want to control their own lives. People do things for selfish reasons, no matter what happens to other people.

We need to understand that God did not make a list of things we must do and things we must not do so He can have a way to test if we obey or not. God gave His laws because He cares for everyone. To understand why God wants us to do some things is sometimes hard. When we understand it is from Him and not what some man thought up, we have the responsibility to obey God's law. We obey because God gives us the command. We are foolish if we do not follow God's law because we think it is not important. We are showing a bad pride if we do not follow God's law because we think we live in a different time and do not need His law. We are showing we do not care for God's knowledge.

Satan: the Enemy of Humankind

Satan is like a person. He is fully evil. He is leading sin in this world. We do believe Satan is real. He is powerful. Believing these things about Satan does not make people have less responsibility for their sin. We cannot be silly and forget about the punishment that comes from sin by joking and saying, "The devil made me do it." The Bible is clear. It says we must stay away from Satan. The Bible says God gave us the power to stay away from Satan. (See Jas. 1:13-16.)

Satan has many names in the New Testament. He is called Satan, the accuser, the tempter, the destroyer, the evil one, the enemy, the old serpent, the prince of the world, Beelzebub, and Belial. He is also called a liar and a murderer. The Bible shows Satan is responsible for sin. The Bible shows that through demons Satan can make sickness, problems, strange actions, and death.

The Book of Revelation talks a lot about Satan. That book shows how fully sin comes from him. Satan does all he can to trick Christians and other people. But one day Satan will be destroyed. He is not in control of this world. It sometimes looks as if Satan controls the world, but he does not. God controls the world.

PERSONAL LEARNING ACTIVITY 3

T F 1. The Bible shows that humans are the highest part of all God made.

T F 2. Man is made in God's image, but woman is made in man's image.

T F 3. The soul is separate from the body; so, what the body does cannot hurt the soul.

T F 4. A person is one being. He is made up of body, soul, and spirit.

T F 5. Any belief that thinks one race of people is better than another is in conflict with what the Bible teaches.

T F 6. God commanded men and women to rule over the earth. That means we can use the earth any way we wish.

T F 7. Christians are concerned about the careful balance in nature (ecology) because Christians believe all the world belongs to God.

T F 8. Baptist have always believed that each person has the right to choose Christ or not choose Him.

T F   9. If someone believes in original sin, that does not mean he must believe a person is lost because of inherited sin.

T F   10. Satan is real in the world and bad. Therefore, people are not responsible for their sin.

Answers: 1. T, 2. F, 3. F, 4. T, 5. T, 6. F, 7. T, 8. T, 9. T, 10. F

CHAPTER 4

The Doctrine of Christ

*In the past God spoke to our ancestors many times and
in many ways through the prophets, but in these last
days he has spoken to us through his Son. He is the
one through whom God created the universe, the one
whom God has chosen to possess all things at the end.
He reflects the brightness of God's glory and is the exact likeness of God's own being, sustaining the universe
with his powerful word. After achieving forgiveness for
the sins of mankind, he sat down in heaven at the
right side of God, the Supreme Power.*
Hebrews 1:1-3 (GNB)

A little bit more than 100 years after Jesus
lived on earth, a man from Rome named
Pliny wrote this prayer: "Oh, God, won't you show us what you
intended the world to be? Won't you show us some way what
purpose you had for us? Could not you give us a perfect example?" Hebrews 1:1-3 is the answer for Pliny's question. These
verses tell us that God did speak in the past. God spoke in many
ways. God spoke to us by Jesus. These verses tell us God gave
Jesus control (heir) of all things. These verses say Jesus made the
whole world. These verses tell us Jesus shows us exactly what
God is like. Jesus makes it possible for our sins to be cleaned
away. After Jesus made it possible for our sins to be cleaned
away, Jesus sat down at the right side of God. Peter told us this
was God's plan from the beginning: "He had been chosen by
God before the creation of the world and was revealed in these
last days for your sake" (1 Pet. 1:20, GNB).

The word *reveal* means to show. God reveals Himself to people. God shows Himself to people. God showed Himself to people in Jesus. Jesus reveals God to people. God revealed Himself in many ways. God spoke His word to the world. In all the ways God spoke, He was making the world ready to hear His last word—Jesus. All the ways God revealed Himself before Jesus were part of the full revelation of God. The Hebrew language uses two pictures to explain that Jesus is the perfect revelation of God.

The first picture is that Jesus is "the brightness of God's glory" (Heb. 1:3). Jesus is the shining glory of God. Jesus comes to us from God just as light shines from the sun. Wise Jewish people who studied about God wrote about God's shining glory. They often used the Hebrew language word *shekinah*.

The word *shekinah* was the brightness of God in the cloud by day and the fire by night. The brightness of God led the Hebrew people from the wilderness. *Shekinah* was the word in the Hebrew language used to describe Moses' face. Moses' face was shining when he came down from the mountain. Moses' face was shining so brightly that Moses had to cover his face with a cover. The *shekinah* shining of God meant that God was there. God's *shekinah* shining glory was seen when Jesus was changed (transfigured) on the mountain. Jesus is where God is. Jesus is the shining light of God.

Jesus: God in Human Body (Incarnation)

We use the word *incarnation* to talk about Jesus. God became a man in Jesus. God was in human body. That is what *incarnation* means. Before God made the world, God decided that He would come down to this earth and live in the world He had made. God decided He would come as a little baby born into a family. He would live as a poor person in a simple home. He would live in a time when the Jewish people were under the power of Rome. While He was on earth, the devil would tempt Jesus; but He would live a perfect life. Jesus would show people what to do and how to live. For three years He would walk through the little country of Judea. He would tell everyone about the love of God. In the end He would show the love of God by dying on the cross for all who would believe. He would win over death and sin by rising from the dead.

Paul talked about when God became a man (the incarnation) when he wrote, "The attitude you should have is the one that Christ Jesus had: He always had the nature of God, but he did not think that by force he should try to become equal with God. Instead of this, of his own free will he gave up all he had, and took the nature of a servant. He became like man and appeared in human likeness" (Phil. 2:5-7, GNB). Jesus became a man. Jesus was limited as a man. Jesus limited Himself so He could do what was needed to save people.

Jesus made the whole world (universe). Jesus was the way God made all things. (See John 1:1-3; Heb. 1:10.) Jesus was not just made by God when Jesus came to earth as a baby. Jesus was the person of God who made the whole world and all that is in the world. Jesus is God. Jesus made each of us to be people who are one of a kind (unique). Jesus knows each thing about us that is different. That thought makes us feel good. He knows us, and He still loves us.

Jesus lives forever. Jesus never changes. (See Heb. 1:11-12.) The world keeps going toward its end. All things get old and wear out. But Jesus does not change. Jesus is the same in the past, today, and forever in the future. (See Heb. 13:8.) In the Gospels of Matthew, Mark, Luke, and John we see that Jesus loved the people and cared for them. He does not change. He still understands the needs of people. He still cares for people. He still has mercy for people.

Jesus: Born of a Virgin
In the New Testament the books of Matthew and Luke tell the story of the birth of Jesus. Those books say that Jesus' mother, Mary, was a virgin. *Virgin* means a person who has not had sexual relationships. John understood about Jesus' birth. (See John 1:14.) So did Paul. (See Gal. 4:4.) Many people who believe in Jesus think the Bible is God's Word that He gave to us. For those people the few verses listed above are enough to help them believe in the virgin birth of Jesus.

Some people have more free beliefs (liberal beliefs). Some of these people are not sure Jesus had a virgin birth. When someone does not believe the virgin birth of Jesus, it is easy to then believe Jesus was not God, that He was not divine. The Christian religion has always believed in the virgin birth of Jesus. The Bible does not say a person must believe in the virgin birth to be saved. People who come to Christ do not start thinking all of a sudden about the virgin birth of Jesus. But as he studies the Bible, he will see what the Bible says about the virgin birth. When a person sees in the Bible that Jesus is God, then that person can accept the idea of the virgin birth of Jesus. If that person refuses to believe, he is not accepting what the Bible says about Jesus. If a person does not believe what the Bible says about Jesus' birth, then that person may stop believing other things the Bible teaches. The Bible clearly teaches that God is Jesus' Father. The Bible teaches that Jesus' life began inside His mother because of the Holy Spirit (Matt. 1:18). What we believe about the virgin birth of Jesus is important. This belief teaches us that Jesus is an only one-of-a-kind (unique) Son of God.

Jesus: the Supreme Revelation

There are many groups that use the name *Christian*, but they really do not follow right beliefs. Groups like this are called *cults*. If you want to test the beliefs of a group to see if it might be a cult group, the first test you use is to ask that group what it believes about Jesus. Many cult groups have ideas about Jesus that are not like what the Bible says about Jesus. A group like this believes that some other idea about Jesus is more important than what the Bible says about Jesus. It does not matter if a cult group says it follows Jesus. If the cult group does not believe that Jesus shows fully what God is like, that group teaches false things.

We ask a cult group an important question: What do you believe about Jesus? Any group that says some added revelation about God has come after Jesus is a cult. God has already shown Himself finally and *fully* in Jesus. The Book of Hebrews in the New Testament makes clear that Jesus shows (reveals) God in a perfect way. Paul wrote, "For the full content of divine nature lives in Christ, in his humanity" (Col. 2:9, GNB).

Jesus said, "I am the way, the truth, and the life; no one goes to the Father except by me" (John 14:6, GNB). Philip said, "Lord, show us the Father; that is all we need" (John 14:8, GNB). Jesus said in the next verse, "For a long time I have been with you all; yet you do not know me, Philip?" What this teaches is clear. Anyone who has seen Jesus has seen the Father. To look and look for God is not needed. God is here in Jesus Christ and no other place. If you want to see what God's glory is like, look to Jesus. If you want to know the healing of God, look to Jesus. If you want to learn how much God cares, look to Jesus. If you want to go into God's kingdom, look to Jesus. If you want to study what God is like, look to Jesus.

Jesus is "the exact likeness of God's own being" (Heb. 1:3, GNB). Jesus is like a picture of God. In the first 100 years after Jesus lived, often the king would print his face on one side of a coin and some message to the people on the other side of the coin. This was a way to help the people understand what the king was like. If the king wanted the people to think he was kind, he would print his face on one side of the coin. He would print the picture of a god who was kind on the other side of the coin. The king would build statues all over the kingdom, showing himself the way he wanted the people to think about him. The people who read the Book of Hebrews knew about images printed on coins and other places to show what the king was like. Jesus is like this. Jesus shows the image of God. Jesus showed in a perfect way what God wants us to know about Himself.

One reason why Baptists do not think it is right to use statues (images) is because nothing people make can show God better than the way Jesus shows God. Any time people try to show God with an image, they do not praise Him; they bring Him down. A statue built by people does not help worship. A statue like this makes our eyes look at the statue instead of looking at Jesus. Jesus is the only image of God we should study. We do not find God pictured in His servants, no matter how good they may be in preaching or leading. We do not find God truly shown in paintings or statues. We find God in Jesus Christ.

John 1:1 says Jesus is the Word. Jesus is what God says to the world. He is the final and full thing God says to the world. God will never say more to the world than what He has said in Jesus.

When we hear a word, we get an idea in our mind. Words like *ice, fire, daughter, grandson,* and *paycheck* put a clear idea in our mind. When we hear the name *Jesus*, what God is like should come into our mind.

Jesus: Prophet, Priest, and King

Jesus came to this earth as a prophet, priest, and king to do three kinds of work. As a prophet, Jesus shows God to people and explains God to people. Working as a prophet, Jesus taught His disciples that Jesus is the way, the truth, and the life. (See John 14:6.) Jesus did wonderful things that can only be done with God's power. Jesus did miracles. Jesus told stories full of wonderful truth. Jesus told parables. The miracles Jesus did and the parables Jesus told showed the right way of life. Jesus always was helping His disciples have a better understanding of what the kingdom of God really is. Jesus lived His life always in the truth. Everything He did, every word He said, and His death for the sins for all people showed the truth. As God's prophet, He told the people who followed Him about the future of God's kingdom. After Jesus died and rose from the dead, He showed more new true things to the people who followed Him.

Jesus also did the work of a priest. We will talk more about this kind of work later. His work as a priest is to offer His life to God; to make sacrifice. Also, He works to bring God and people together.

As a king, Jesus is ruler over all. Jesus came to earth the first time. He made His Kingdom. Jesus said He had the right of ruler because He was the Messiah. *Messiah* means the person God promised to the world. Jesus told the people they must fully obey Him. Jesus spoke with full power. Jesus did miracles. Jesus set up His church. Jesus set up baptism and the Lord's Supper. Jesus died on a cross. Jesus won over death. Jesus went up to the right hand of God. Jesus will rule as king until all His enemies lose. Jesus sends His followers to preach the good news to the world. Jesus speaks to God for His people. He sends His Spirit to fill the church with power. Jesus will come again to take His people who will rule with Him forever and ever.

Jesus: Divine and Human

We talked about how Jesus is God in chapter 2. Jesus is God. He is man. He is God-man. As God, He shows God to us in a perfect way. As man, He shows man to God in a perfect way. Jesus said to His disciples, "Whoever has seen me has seen the Father" (John 14:9, GNB). He said, "The Father and I are one" (John 10:30, GNB). Other verses in the Bible show that Jesus saw Himself as the only one-of-a-kind Son to God the Father: Matthew 11:25-27; Mark 12:35-37; 13:32; and 14:61-64. Other New Testament verses (too many to list) show how much power Jesus had over the world, the demons, the Bible, and forgiveness of sins. But a person must have faith to believe Jesus Christ is God Himself. The Bible shows proofs for what Jesus said about Himself. These proofs are the miracles Jesus did, His death, and His rising from the grave. However, a person can be sure about Jesus only by faith. We must experience Christ by meeting Him and by knowing we have really met God.

Jesus was God (divine). Jesus was human. But we should use the word to talk about Jesus. Jesus *is* divine. Jesus *is* human. Jesus will be divine and human forever. Because He is divine and human forever, He always understands us as humans. (See Heb. 4:14-16.) Maybe the verses that best show Jesus as a man is the story about Jesus' time of temptation in the wilderness in Matthew 4:1-11. (See also Mark 1:12-13; Luke 4:1-13.)

Jesus was tempted right after He was baptized. The Spirit led Jesus into the wilderness. The word *led* has the idea of forced. Jesus was still under God's leading in this temptation time, just as He was under God's leading when He was baptized. This temptation time was important in the life and work of Jesus. No one saw Jesus while He was tempted. Jesus must have told His disciples about it because it was important.

The Bible tells the reason why Jesus had this experience "to be tempted by the Devil" (Matt. 4:1, GNB). The English word *tempted* comes from the Greek word *peirazo*. This Greek word is used to mean to try, to prove, to put to the test, or to find out what kind of person someone is. Sometimes it is used to mean to try to trap someone like when the Pharisees tried to trap Jesus. The word is used to mean to try to pull someone into sin. In fact, the name of Satan is a form of this word. We can understand the verse in two ways: (1) Jesus was tested, or (2) Satan tried to pull Jesus into sin.

This is a hard verse to understand. People all through Christian history have used the two ways to explain the verse listed above. The first answer is good in some ways. For one thing, the first answer keeps us from having to think about Jesus as a man and the hard question of whether Jesus was able to sin. On one hand, Hebrews 4:15 says Jesus was tempted in every way just as we are, yet without sin. On the other hand, James 1:13 (GNB) says, "If a person is tempted by such trials, he must not say, 'This temptation comes from God.' For God cannot be tempted by evil, and he himself tempts no one."

God did not tempt Jesus. Satan did the tempting. But Jesus was led by the Spirit into the wilderness for the reason of being tempted. In the Model Prayer a form of a Greek word is used (*peirasmon*, Matt. 6:13). In that prayer Jesus teaches us to pray for God not to lead us into temptation. The idea of this use of the word is that God wants us to grow. If we will grow, then we must go through times of hard decision making. We must go through times when we decide our way or we make big leaps of faith to deeper levels of understanding. We go through times that lead us to give our lives to God. These times are hard and full of danger. At such times, we have choices that might take us the wrong way. We should be careful about such times of testing. We should pray not to have to go through them. The decisions are important. The choices we face can lead to sin and wrong.

Some people began to have false ideas about the person and work of Christ early in Christian history. These ideas said God did not really become a man. These ideas were a part of the teachings known as "gnosticism." The people who taught these ideas did not believe Christ was really human. They could not accept these ideas that God would become part of the worldly things. They thought all the things of this world are full of evil. This false idea taught that Christ only looked like a man and that Jesus only looked like a man for a short time. People who followed this teaching did not believe Jesus Christ really came in the flesh. Many wise people who study the Bible a lot believe some of the New Testament, like John, was written against this false idea.

Through all of Christian history, wise people who study the Bible a lot tried to understand how Jesus could be 100 percent God and 100 percent human at the same time. It is true that this idea does not seem right in human ways. But it is true, and that is part of the mystery of Jesus. The Bible shows Jesus is both fully God and fully human. We try to explain what the Bible says. The way we explain this is just a human try to understand something that cannot be fully explained.

In some way, Jesus emptied Himself when He came to earth. (See Phil. 2:6-8.) We do not know what all that means. What happened after Jesus emptied Himself is that He truly suffered and died. What happened after Jesus emptied Himself is that He truly became hungry and tired. He was really tempted to sin.

Jesus: the Promised Messiah

The word *Messiah* means anointed one. When the nation of Israel was young, the person who was the anointed one was the human leader. These were people like David. God chose David. Later, God used the idea of Messiah to show that one day the perfect leader would come and save the nation of Israel from its enemies. God began to tell Israel through the prophets about the Anointed One—the Messiah—who would come later. The prophets used two ideas when they preached about this coming Messiah. First, the prophets said that the Messiah was to be a great King who would lead Israel to become the nation who would rule the world. Second, the prophets said the Messiah was to be a Suffering Servant.

The Jews understood and believed the first idea about the Messiah. The Jews did not understand or believe the second idea about the Messiah. During the time between the close of the Old Testament and the beginning of the New Testament (this time is called the interbiblical period), a group of writings called the *Apocrypha* were written. An idea about a Messiah who would be a government leader is in these writings. The Jews fully accepted the idea of the Messiah as a government leader and an army leader before Jesus was born (the first century). The verses in the Old

Testament that showed the Messiah as a Suffering Servant were misunderstood. The Jews thought those verses were only talking about the whole nation of Israel and not one person.

The Jews were looking for the Messiah to come in the time when Jesus lived. Jesus did come. He understood the verses that talk about the Suffering Servant. Jesus knew He was the Suffering Servant. These Suffering Servant verses talk about a Messiah who is different from the Messiah the Jews were looking for. The men who led the Jewish religion during Jesus' time would not accept the way Jesus explained the Messiah. They would not accept a Suffering Servant.

We learn about Jesus as a man when we study His temptations. We also learn about Jesus the Messiah when we study His temptations. God led Jesus into the wilderness when Jesus was beginning His work on earth. Jesus decided for sure He would be a Suffering Servant Messiah.

Satan tempted Jesus to change the stone into bread. (See Matt. 4:3-4.) Jesus would be a Messiah who would work to meet the selfish needs of other people if He used His power in a selfish way to make bread to eat. He would have to become a Messiah who made bread for the people if He fell to this temptation. His main work would have become taking care of the bodily needs of people. People would not have a deep desire to follow a Messiah like that. People would follow Jesus for wrong reasons. History has already shown the bread way is wrong. God did great things to free Israel from slavery. God fed them by a wonderful work in the wilderness. They became unfaithful to God as soon as they forgot about God's wonderful work. What God gave was not enough. They got bread. They wanted other food. The nature of a kingdom is built on selfish needs. Jesus did not seek that kind of kingdom.

In the second temptation (see Matt. 4:5-7), Satan took Jesus to the high corner of the Temple. Some people think this place was the southeast corner of the mountain that looks out over the Kidron Valley. But it seems that this was on the Temple and looked over the Temple yard. Some of the Jews thought when the Messiah came He would show Himself first in the Temple yard. Maybe that would be an easy way for Jesus to begin His work. He

could follow the temptation and jump from the high Temple corner with all the people seeing Him. Jesus was tempted to do this
at the Temple yard and have the people see angels catch Him
before His body hit the hard stones.

During Jesus' first year of work, not many people knew about
Him. Not much is written in the Bible about that first year. Jesus
was in Judea most of that year. He was not in Galilee. Jesus was in
Galilee most of the time the last two years. Why should Jesus
have one whole year without the people knowing much about
Him? He could start His work with a big show at the Temple.
People would know right away that He said He was the Messiah.
The people would have come from everywhere to hear Him
speak. Is this true? Maybe the people would only come to see
Him do more tricks and miracles. Jesus saw all the meaning of
the temptation. Jesus would not make Himself a show-off Messiah. No one would hear His words if Jesus did that. They would
only want to see His miracles.

The third temptation was for Jesus to fall down and worship
Satan. (See Matt. 4:8-9.) Satan surely was bold! Jesus came to
earth to be the king of the people. Satan used that idea to try to
get Jesus. Jesus came to save the world. Satan promised Jesus
could have the world in an easy way. How do you think Satan
could have given Jesus the world? Satan would have won if Jesus
worshiped Satan. Jesus was God in flesh. Satan would be God if
Jesus worshiped Satan. Satan would have become His master.

Alexander the Great lived 300 years before Christ. Alexander's father started the war to win all of Greece. Alexander became the king. It took Alexander 13 years to win all the world
from Greece to the edge of India. Satan said he could do that for
Jesus.

Many wise people think in this temptation Satan was trying to
get Jesus to become an army-leading Messiah. Jesus would do
what the Jews thought the Messiah would do if He did that.
Later, just after Peter said Jesus was the Son of the living God,
Peter said Jesus would not be killed. Jesus said He would be
killed. Peter said no. (See Matt. 16:21-23.) Jesus answered Peter
in a hard way. We must understand that Peter was thinking Jesus
would be an army-leading Messiah. Peter was making the same

temptation as the third temptation from Satan. Jesus had already decided He would not be a Messiah like that.

The people tried to make Jesus king after He fed the 5,000 people. (See John 6:14-15.) The people wanted an army-leading Messiah. They really wanted Jesus because He could feed them when they were hungry! If Jesus became an army-leading Messiah, then that would break everything Jesus taught about being a servant.

Jesus asked His disciples, "Who do you say I am?" (Matt. 16:15, GNB). Peter answered for the group: "You are the Messiah, the Son of the living God" (Matt. 16:16, GNB). The word *Christ* is the Greek language word that means the same as the Hebrew language word *Messiah*. *Christ* and *Messiah* mean the same thing. God gave this answer to the disciples. This answer is more than a human can understand. Jesus then told the disciples they must not tell any one that He was the Messiah. (See Matt. 16:20.) Jesus was not keeping the news quiet. He was trying to stop the people from believing the wrong things about the Messiah. The people had the wrong idea about that word. The people expected a government leader and an army-leading Messiah. That is why Jesus did not use the word often.

Jesus liked to use the words *Son of man*. These words were from the Book of Daniel. These words were talking about the Messiah. Jesus gave these words the meaning He wanted. The way Jesus lived as Messiah surprised everyone. He was a Messiah who was a savior. He was a Messiah who broke down the things that separate different kinds of people, different ways of living, different sexes, different languages. He was a Savior for all people everywhere.

Jesus: the High Priest

The Jews did not think just any person could meet straight (person to person) with God. In the Temple was a place called the holy of holies. That was a place only the high priest could go in. The high priest could only go in that place one time each year on the Day of Atonement. He could only go in that place after he made a sacrifice for his own sins and for the sins of the people. The priest killed an animal for the sacrifice. The sacrifice took away the sin that separated God and His people.

The person who wrote the Book of Hebrews said sin did not have to separate people from God. Hebrews 10:19-22 tells about the new and living way people can go near to God. In the past, a sinful man (the priest) made a sacrifice for sinful people. The priest would sacrifice a lamb and put it on the altar of God before God. But sin was still always there. There was never a perfect priest who could bring a perfect sacrifice for sin. But Jesus is the Great High Priest. Jesus does not have any sin. Jesus is perfect in every way.

The wall of sin that separated people from God is no longer there. Because Jesus sacrificed His own life and because Jesus is a priest for us, every man, woman, and child on earth can go straight to God. There is not any place in a Temple called the holy of holies any more. There is no Day of Atonement. There is no blood sacrifices. None of that is needed any more because of Jesus. Jesus was our perfect sacrifice. He is our perfect High Priest. Now we can go straight to God. We can go into God's presence.

Jesus Christ is like a bridge for us. We can go over that bridge to God Himself. We can have full forgiveness for sin. We can be fully clean from sin. We can have full salvation. People who believe in Jesus wait for the time when Jesus will come again. The perfect Savior (Jesus) will take us to the perfect heaven Jesus made for us.

Hebrews 7:1-17 talks about a man in the Old Testament named Melchizedek. Melchizedek was a man who was a king and a priest at the same time Abraham lived. The writer of Hebrews talks about the *priesthood* of Melchizedek. We do not know anything about Melchizedek's parents. We do not know anything about his death. He lived on earth long before the Hebrew priesthood was set up by God. Abraham made sacrifice to Melchizedek. Abraham paid tithes through him. A tithe is one-tenth of what you have.

The Book of Hebrews uses Melchizedek as an example to tell some things about Jesus' priesthood. Melchizedek lived on earth before the Old Testament priesthood started. Jesus' priesthood is older and even greater. In the Old Testament, the priests all came from the Levi family. Jesus is not from the Levi family. Melchizedek is not from the Levi family. Jesus is a priest. Melchizedek was a priest. Both Jesus and Melchizedek do not have a beginning and do not have an end. Both have God's blessing before the Hebrew priests began.

Jesus is a promise to us that the New Testament, which shows what God wants for His people now, is better than the old. (See Heb. 7:22.) The Bible tells us that human priests die. Jesus lives forever. (See Heb. 7:23-24.) Jesus now is at the right hand of God. (See Heb. 1:3.) What is Jesus doing at the right hand of God? Jesus is not judging against us. No! Jesus is not our Judge. He is our Mediator. *Mediator* means Jesus is standing between God and us. He is talking with God on our behalf. Jesus works between us and God right now and at the end of time. He talks to the Father for those people who believe in Jesus. The people who are saved by His blood come under Jesus' care.

Hebrews 4:14-16 tell in a few words what the whole Book of Hebrews is saying. The writer says, "Turn your eyes upon Jesus." These verses say we have a *great* High Priest. The Greek language word for *great* is *megan*. This word means the greatest. There is no great greater than *megan*. *Gone through* (v. 14) means something that is finished. Jesus finished His work. He is now one with God, where He shall be forever. We find the word *sympathize* in verse 15. The Greek language word here means to feel what someone else feels and not just to know about what someone else feels. We have a High Priest who experienced everything we feel.

John Foster was a government worker for Britain. He lived in China before World War II. Foster had to leave China when the Japanese army came into China. One day he came home. He checked his teenage daughter. She was listening to the news on the radio. The news said Japanese tanks moved into Canton, China. The daughter began to cry. Then she started to cry real hard. Her body started to shake from hard crying. Foster remembered that many people heard the news, but few were hurt by the news the way she was. Why? Because she was born there. She lived there. She went to school there. Her nurses, teachers, and friends were there. She knew the streets and stores. She was hurt more than other people because she had lived there. Hebrews tells us Jesus is like that. Jesus has been there. He understands our feelings, our pains, and our way of life.

Jesus: Lord and King

The early Christians said "Jesus is Lord." These words are found in the New Testament. These words were the first words showing, in a short way, what the Christians believed. Paul helped the Christians at the church in the town of Corinth. He told them to remember that the important test was for people to stay in the fellowship of the church. He told them to let Jesus be the Lord in their lives (1 Cor. 12:3). The word *Lord* is used in all the books of the New Testament except Titus and the letters of John. Christ took the name *Lord* for Himself in Matthew 7:21-22; 22:41-45. When Thomas saw the scars in Jesus' hands after Jesus rose from the grave, Thomas said, "My Lord and my God!" (John 20:28).

America had a great revival in the 1700s. This revival was called the Great Awakening. That revival happened because Christians started preaching about some doctrines that had been forgotten. A great revival later happened when Charles Finney started preaching about the need for people to repent and to accept the forgiveness given at the cross of Jesus. The next great revival talked a lot about prayer and God's power to answer people's prayers.

God used Dwight Moody as the leader of the next revival. That revival talked a lot about the idea of God's love for sinners. Each of these revivals focused attention on some Christian doctrine that people were forgetting. The lordship of Christ is forgotten today. Maybe the next great revival will happen when we start preaching about the doctrine of the lordship of Christ. We will give the Holy Spirit a chance to speak to us through His Word when we study this doctrine. From this study, the Lord may choose to bring revival to our world.

The New Testament often talks about Jesus as Lord. He is called "only Ruler, the King of kings and the Lord of lords" (1 Tim. 6:15, GNB). Pilate asked Jesus, "Are you the king of the Jews?" (John 18:33). Jesus answered, "My kingdom does not belong to this world" (John 18:36). Pilate then said, "Are you a king, then?" (John 18:37). Jesus answered, "You are right in saying I am a king."

Hebrews 1:2 tells us that God made Jesus heir of all things. God put the whole world in Jesus' control. (See Ps. 2:8; Eph. 1:10.) The early church believed Jesus controlled the Kingdom and the whole world. That was part of what the early church preached.

Christ is Lord over all the angels (Heb. 1:4-6). The Jews thought a lot about angels. The Jews thought angels had great power and importance. But the writer of the Book of Hebrews helped the Jews remember that the angels are only servants of Jesus. Angels are sent out by Jesus to do God's work in this world.

Hebrews 1:3 shows Jesus as ruler of the Kingdom. But, what is this Kingdom like? After Jesus arose from the dead, His disciples asked, "Lord, will you at this time give the kingdom back to Israel?" (Acts 1:6, GNB). We must not misunderstand Jesus' answer. Jesus told His disciples clearly that their job was not to know the times or dates the Father set by His own authority (Acts 1:7). They were to stop thinking about the government-power idea of the Kingdom. Jesus meant the disciples would get the power of the Holy Spirit. The disciples would tell about Jesus in the world. They would tell about Jesus in their own home country and in other countries. They would tell all people in all places.

Luke wrote about when Jesus went into heaven. Luke said, "As he was blessing them, he departed from them and was taken up into heaven" (Luke 24:51, GNB). After the blessing, they saw Jesus go up. (See Acts 1:9.) It was important that the disciples saw Jesus do this. They knew and we know for all time where Jesus went. He went to heaven. Heaven is His home. It will be our home. The Kingdom Jesus talked about was a heavenly kingdom. It was not a kingdom of earthly power and money. The capital of God's kingdom was not Jerusalem on earth but Jerusalem in heaven. Jesus went up to be with His Father. This showed the people who follow Jesus that Jesus is one with the Father. This showed Jesus is Kings of kings and Lord of lords. This showed His work of saving people was finished. This showed Jesus was going to His glory.

God took Jesus up in a cloud. God took Jesus to His throne where He rules. Jesus is again at the right hand of His Father. That is where His place is. Christ is on His throne and is making His kingdom ready to give it to the Father when the end comes. We should become excited enough to sing the "Hallelujah Chorus"! Jesus is and will be King of kings and Lord of lords. All things will be finished at the end of the world. We are serving with Jesus to prepare His kingdom. All this is done through His power and wisdom (1 Cor. 15:24-26).

Christ is working in this world. Some day at "the name of Jesus all beings in heaven, on earth, and in the world below will fall on their knees, and all will openly proclaim that Jesus Christ is Lord, to the glory of God the Father" (Phil. 2:10-11, GNB). Jesus is "sustaining [taking care of] the universe with his powerful word" (Heb. 1:3, GNB). He is the A to Z, the first, the last, and all in between. There has never been one minute when God left this world alone. Jesus is always helping to keep the whole world right. (See Col. 1:16-17.) When the Bible talks about thrones, powers, rulers, and authorities, this shows Jesus continues to be working in the things that happen in this world. Jesus spoke— and demons came out, people became well, sin was forgiven, the fig tree died. That same power moves people and nations today.

PERSONAL LEARNING ACTIVITY 4

Read Hebrews 4:14-16.
1. Look in verse 14 to find who is our Great High Priest.

---

2. What do you think verse 15 means? Verse 15 says Jesus was "tempted in every way that we are."

---

3. How does Jesus make us feel good when we need mercy and grace?

CHAPTER 5

The Atoning Work of Christ

He has appeared once and for all, to remove sin
through the sacrifices of himself.
Hebrews 9:26 (GNB)

C hristians have always been interested in the atonement. The word *atonement* is some-times explained for people by breaking the word down like this: at-one-ment. *At-one* here has the idea of bringing people who are separated from God back to God. *Atonement* means what God did to bring people out of sin and back to Himself. God brought people back to Himself through the death of Jesus on the cross. But we must think about this question: How did the death of Jesus on the cross make it so we can come back to God? How did the death of Jesus on the cross make atonement happen? Many wise people who study the Bible a lot tried to explain this. They had different ideas to try to explain this. None of the ideas people had can fully explain the atonement.

Wise people who study the Bible a lot agree about this: The cross is the most important part of the Christian story. What Christ did on the cross was good enough for the sin of all people. God's love was the reason behind the cross. God planned the cross. God made it happen. God made sure it was fully finished. God honors it. God loved all people more than we can under-stand. We were separated from God because of sin. That made real pain for God. God did something to stop the sin problem. If someone has an idea about the atonement and that idea does not include God's love, then that idea is not good enough. God's love for people was the most important reason for the work of

Jesus on the cross—the atonement.

Before time began, God already decided how He wanted to touch the hearts of people with His love. God planned for Jesus to come to the earth before the world began. (See 1 Pet. 1:20.) God planned before He made the world that people who believe in Jesus would be saved because Jesus came. (See Eph. 1:4.)

Sin stopped people from coming back to God. That was a problem that needed to be solved. God is holy. He hates sin. God judges against sin. Sin had to be removed for God and people to come back together. Some people show that God is angry against sin. He judges sin. But, at the same time, God is love and has mercy. This seems to show that God has two different natures in Him that fight each other. This idea can help us to understand the atonement. It shows God must judge sin. It shows God's mercy saves people. But the idea is not fully right. God does not fight with Himself. A human parent loves a child who does wrong, even when the parent must punish the child. The parent does not have two different natures that are fighting inside. The parent is just one person who wants the best for the child, even when the child does wrong. God is just one Person, too. He never stops loving us, even when we are sinful. It was God's love that found a way to solve the sin problem in a way that is both loving and punishes wrong.

There are many different words that talk about the work of Christ in atonement. No one word can fully explain the word *atonement*. What Jesus did to take away our sin (atonement) and the changes that happen in a person's life are so many that many different words must be used to explain this. Some of the words that explain the atonement are big words, but they are good words to learn. They each teach great truths.

Christ's Atonement: Substitution

The word *substitution* means for one thing to take the place of another thing. For example, you might use a low calorie sweetener in the place of sugar. The sweetener took the place of the sugar. You substituted sweetener for sugar. Christ was killed on the cross as a substitute for us. Christ took our place on the cross.

The word *substitute* is not found in the Bible in the verses that talk about atonement. But, several verses teach the truth about substitution. Romans 3:24-26 has three important atonement words: *justified* (put right), *redemption* (sets free), and *sacrifice* (Christ's death). The main idea of the verses is that Christ died in our place. Mark 10:45 talks about a *ransom*. This verse means that since Christ died, we do not die. Paul wrote that Jesus was made to be sin for us. (See 2 Cor. 5:21.) Sin was made a curse for us. (See Gal. 3:13.) Some people today have a hard time accepting the idea that one Person can really take another person's punishment. The New Testament is clear in these and other verses. Jesus' death was in our place. His death was a substitution for ours. If His death was not a substitution, then the sin problem is not yet solved.

Christ's Atonement: Covenant

Many Christians do not understand the idea of covenant very well. The word *covenant* means an agreement that God makes with people. Most of the time when we talk about covenant in our churches we think about believers in Jesus making a covenant together as they start a church. This means the people make some promises to one another and to Christ. The word can mean this. But it means a lot more as it is used in the Bible. We need to understand covenant so we can understand Jesus' atonement.

There is a difference between covenant and promise in the Bible. The Bible talks about many promises, but it only talks about a few covenants. The first covenant in the Bible is the covenant God made with Noah. An important part of the covenant was that the covenant was made to help all people, not just one nation. (See Gen. 9:9-10,12,15-17.) This covenant shows us that God's plan in history is for all people. God made more covenants. We will look at those covenants next. God planned to use these covenants as ways to reach all people.

The next covenant we will talk about is God's covenant with Abraham. God said His reason for this covenant was so that "through you I will bless all the nations" (Gen. 12:3, GNB). In the covenant Abraham was to be the father of a nation. God planned to teach that nation and use that nation to reach out to all people everywhere. But many times we see in the Old Testament that Israel failed to understand what God chose Israel for.

The third covenant was the covenant made at Mount Sinai. In this covenant God made the Hebrew people into a nation. God gave them the responsibility to show the world God's ways and laws. God wanted Israel to obey His laws and do His will. If Israel would obey God's laws and do His will, then the people would show all the world how good life would be if people lived the way God wanted. But the people of Israel did not do their part of the Sinai covenant. The people of Israel wanted a king to rule over them in God's place. God gave the people of Israel Samuel to lead them. The people told Samuel they wanted a king. They wanted Samuel to pick a king. (See 1 Sam. 8:4-5.) Samuel did not want to do this. Samuel saw that if the people took a king then they were giving up God as their King. God told Samuel, "You are not the one they have rejected; I am the one they have rejected as their king" (1 Sam. 8:7, GNB). Soon after that, Samuel picked Saul to be Israel's first king.

David was the next king after Saul. God made a promise to David that someone in David's family line would rule over God's people forever. (See 2 Sam. 7:11-16.) This promise became true when Jesus came to earth. Jesus was the Messiah. (See Luke 1:32-33.)

The Sinai covenant and the covenant with David are hard to work together. The Sinai covenant said that only God was king. The covenant with David promised a king from David's family line forever. Only in Jesus Christ could these two different covenants work together. They work together in Jesus because Jesus is God (no king rules between God and His people) and Jesus is in the family line of David (who, as King of kings, rules forever over God's people).

The covenants in the Old Testament had a problem. Those covenants did not give people the inner power needed to obey the covenants. The law helped, but it was not enough. Jeremiah was an Old Testament prophet. He said God would write His law in the hearts of people. (See Jer. 31:33-34.) This became true in the new covenant that is made by Jesus' atoning death. Jesus died. Now all who believe in Jesus are right with God. God brings those people back to Himself. This new covenant gives people power inside their lives to live for God. This power does not come from obeying the law. This power comes from a free, saved friendship with God through Christ.

Christ's Atonement: Sacrifice

Not long ago I read a long story about India. In the story I saw the many different ways the people worship. The people in that great country often worship by making sacrifices. They worship many gods and female gods (goddesses). Part of their worship is to have a party remembering the marriages of the gods. They believe the Ganges River is holy. They think the river can heal sick people. People in India are looking for something to save them from sin and to give them hope and peace.

As in India, people all over the world are looking for something that will save them from their sins. People are looking for something that will give them hope and peace in their lives. People can be saved from sin and can find peace through the good news about Jesus Christ. Hebrews 7:25 (GNB) says "And so he is able . . . to save those who come to God through him, because he lives forever to plead with God for them."

Jesus did not die because He wanted to punish people. Jesus died to save people fully. It does not matter who people are, what they have done in the past, or what they believed in the past. Jesus can fully and totally save a person in every way. Jesus wants to save everyone on earth. Jesus wants to save everyone.

When Jesus died on the cross, He did His work as a priest. Jesus did not sin Himself. But on the cross He took the sin of all people to Himself. When people are joined with Christ through salvation, those people start a new life. In the end of time, those people will be like Christ without sin. When Jesus died on the cross, God, who is holy love, won over sin through Jesus' death (sacrifice).

When Jesus first died, the disciples thought all was lost. They were sad and depressed until Jesus rose from the grave. The disciples opened their hearts to Jesus after He rose from the grave. They understood what Jesus taught. They understood what Jesus had done for them. (See Luke 24:45-47.)

If we want to understand fully the importance of what Jesus

did, then we must study sacrifice in the Old Testament. We cannot make this book too long, so we will only talk about four kinds of sacrifice. We will talk about *burnt* sacrifices, *peace* sacrifices, *sin* sacrifices, and *guilt offering* sacrifices. A man by the name of Leon Morris wrote a book and listed six things that are in all Old Testament sacrifices. These six things are these: (1) going near for worship; (2) putting hands on the sacrifice which showed that a person's sins were given to the sacrifice; (3) the person who was worshiping killed the animal (the priest did not kill the animal), and this showed that the person worshiping was sinful and should die; (4) the blood from the sacrifice was used by the priest and showed that sin was serious; (5) the sacrifice was burned up on the altar, the smoke and smell went up toward God and this was how the offering was made to God; (6) the dead body was taken care of with parts of the body given to different people which showed how the different people were part of the worship.[1]

The Jews who lived in the first 100 years after Jesus knew all these parts of the sacrifice. People who were not Jews (Gentiles) knew these things because Gentile people made sacrifices in their different religions. These different parts of the sacrifice help people understand about Jesus' sacrifice. We must remember that Jesus' sacrifice was different. His sacrifice was perfect. It does not need to be done again and again. Jesus was our sacrifice. Sacrifices are not needed now.

Hebrews 7:26-27 (GNB) talks about Jesus as a priest. It says: "Jesus, then, is the High Priest that meets our needs. He is holy; he has no fault or sin in him; he has been set apart from sinners and raised above the heavens. He is not like the other high priests; he does not need to offer sacrifices every day for his own sins first and then for the sins of the people. He offered one sacrifice, once and for all, when he offered himself." Jesus is holy. No one else needs to try to make a sacrifice pure now. He is without blame. (Greek language word is *akakos* means fully innocent.) He is pure. (Greek language word *amiantos* means to have no uncleanness.) He is separate from sinners. There is no other perfect sacrifice. Jesus is raised in power (exalted). No greater sacrifice will ever be needed. His sacrifice was perfect forever. He was the perfect priest forever. All these things show the difference between Jesus and the earthly Jewish high priest. The Jewish high priest changed often. Those high priests could not save people. Those high priests were only men. They had their own sin like all other people. Their sacrifices were not perfect. They were only good for a short time. Those priests were people with people's problems. Jesus is able to fully save all people who come to Him. (See Heb. 7:25). It does not matter how bad a sinner is. Jesus can save that sinner.

Christ's Atonement: Redemption

Jesus' death redeemed us from sin. *Redeem* means to buy something back. Jesus redeemed us. He bought us back out of sin. Christians are free now from sin. (See Gal. 5:1.) When Jesus lived on earth, slaves were everywhere. A person could be born as a slave. A person could become a slave as a prisoner of war. A person might be kidnapped and sold as a slave. If a person was a slave, then his children also were slaves. Sometimes a person or a group of people would pay money and buy the slave. Then the slave was free. That is the idea of what Jesus did for us. The spiritual idea is that Christ paid for our sin with His blood. What Jesus paid was good enough. Wise people who study the Bible a lot at different times in history have tried to say to whom Jesus paid the price. Thinking like this often does not make the idea more clear. The most important idea in the Bible about redemption is that Christ makes us free. This idea makes clear that God used great power to make us free. God used His great power in Christ to make us free, and nothing else could make us free. Freedom is full in Jesus Christ.

We can understand that Jesus worked to redeem us because of who He was. Paul said, "Believe in the Lord Jesus, and you will be saved" (Acts 16:31, GNB). Jesus did not come to earth only to teach and preach. He came to do something that could only be done on the cross. Jesus said, "The Son of Man came to seek and to save the lost" (Luke 19:10, GNB). On the Day of Pentecost, Peter was talking about Christ. He said, "In accordance with his own plan God had already decided that Jesus would be handed over to you; and you killed him by letting sinful men crucify him" (Acts 2:23, GNB). Paul said, "Christ was without sin, but for our sake God made him share our sin in order that in union with him we might share the righteousness of God" (2 Cor. 5:21, GNB). We are redeemed from sin because Jesus agreed to take our sins in His body so that we might die to sin and live in God's right way. (See 1 Pet. 2:24.)

Why did God let the cross happen? Jesus explained it best when He said, "As Moses lifted up the bronze snake on a pole in the desert, in the same way the Son of Man must be lifted up, so that everyone who believes in him may have eternal life" (John 3:14-15, GNB). Sinners cannot get rid of their own sin. In the cross God did for sinners what they could not do for themselves.

Jesus redeemed us from all sin. All of our sins are forgiven because of His blood.

Christ's Atonement: Reconciliation

T. W. Hunt wrote a book in 1986 named *The Doctrine of Prayer*. In that book he tells a story about talking with a woman about Jesus. Hunt asked her this question, "If Jesus' blood cleans you, how clean can you be?" (p. 62). One time I was preparing for an evangelistic crusade in Dayton, Ohio. I was teaching people who would help in the crusade as counselors. One of the counselors won a young woman to Christ. She brought this young woman to the crusade. The young woman used drugs and could not stop. She had marks on her arms from using shot needles to put drugs in her arms. She also sold her body for sex. Her mother made her start selling her body for sex when she was only 10 years old. When this young woman came to the front at the crusade to tell about accepting Christ, she said: "I've met Jesus today, and He made me clean. I'm no longer dirty and filthy. I'm clean again."

Reconciliation means to bring back together two people who are separated. Christ died to bring people who are separated from God back to God. Christ died to reconcile people to God. We are separated from God because of sin. (See Rom. 5:10.) Christ brought God and people who believed on Jesus into a right relationship. God is not the one who changes. Reconciliation does not mean that God changes so He can come back to us. Sin separates us from God. The sin problem had to be taken care of because God is against sin and all bad things. God made the way to reconciliation. (See Rom. 5:11.) God does not change. We must let God change us. We are brought back to God, not God back to us. (See 2 Cor. 5:18-20; Col. 1:21-22.)

Reconciliation does not mean we need to get better. *Reconciliation* does not mean we need to get religion. *Reconciliation* does not mean we are equal to God. Both of us are separated, and both of us come back. Only God has full control (sovereign). He has the right to judge us. He has made a way to fully change us through a new birth. (See John 3.) *Born again* comes from two Greek language words. The first Greek language word is *gennethe*. This word means is born. The other Greek language word is *anothen*. This word has three meanings. It means from above; from the beginning; and again or renew. Many times in the New Testament we can find the idea of being born again or being made over again. (See Rom. 6:11; Gal, 6:15; Titus 3:5; Jas. 1:18; 1 Pet. 1:3,23; 1 John 2:29; 3:9; 4:7; 5:1,4,18.)

God did not make us to be separated from Him. When God reconciles us, we start to become what God made us to be. We start to be people living at peace with God and at peace with other people. (See Eph. 2:11-21.) Our world is full of problems, angry fighting, and war. Christ is the way to peace. When people are truly reconciled in Christ and when people work to follow what Jesus taught, then true peace comes to our world.

Christ's Atonement: Propitiation/Expiation

This idea is one of the hardest for people to understand. One reason why it is hard to understand is because it is hard to find English words that mean the same as the Greek language word. The Greek language word is *hilasmos*. This word appears in 1 John 2:2; 4:10; and in another form of the word in Romans 3:25. In the King James Version Bible, *propitiation* is the English word used for *hilasmos*. The Revised Standard Version Bible uses *expiation* for *hilasmos*. These two English words are different in meaning. James Hastings edited the *Dictionary of the Bible*. This book was revised by Frederick C. Grant and H. H. Rowley. That book explains the meaning of *propitiation* and *expiation*. You may make someone angry or hurt his honor. If you did something to make his anger go away or did something to satisfy his honor, that is *propitiation*. If you are guilty of doing wrong or sin and then something is done to take away your guilt or sin, that is *expiation*. *Expiation* has the idea of taking away sin. It does not have the idea of satisfying an angry God so He will not be angry. When Jesus lived, many religions used the idea of propitiation. *Expiation* means taking away sin by using a sacrifice. It means that the sin is gone. It is as if the sin never was here in the first place. The *New International Version* of the Bible uses the English words *atoning sacrifice* for the Greek language word *hilasmos* in 1 John. These English words give us the same idea as expiation. These words mean taking away sin by the sacrifice of Jesus on the cross.

This is what Christ's sacrifice does for people who believe in Jesus. The idea in all three verses we talked about above is that Jesus is the atoning sacrifice given by God. The idea is not that Jesus' sacrifice made God stop being an angry God. The idea is that the God of love Himself gave the sacrifice. Christ has provided purification for sins. *Purify* means to make clean. The dirt of sin is gone. Because we are cleaned from sin by the blood of Christ, our sin is taken care of. Now we can come to God without fear. (See Heb. 4:16.) Jesus came to earth and died. He went through death for everyone. (See Heb. 2:9.) That was the reason He came. He came to suffer and die for our sin. The cross is in the middle of God's plan. The cross was the last sacrifice of death. On the cross, the Son of God (who had no sin) died for the sins of all who believe in Him.

Christ's Atonement: Justification

The idea of justification is in the New Testament many times. Most of the time English language Bibles use *justice* or *righteousness* for the Greek word for *justification*. Both of these English words have the right idea. Both ideas of justice and righteousness are part of the Greek idea of *justification*.

Justice means to judge in a right way. *Righteousness* means to live in a right way. Justice must be righteous. Justice comes from a foundation of holiness. Righteousness must make justice happen. In the Old Testament, the prophets spoke for God. God demanded righteousness through the prophets. God's demand for righteousness only came true when there was justice all over the country of Israel. The New Testament shows that justice and righteousness are always together. God is just. He always judges in the right way. That same God justifies us. He judges us and finds us not guilty because of Jesus. God is righteous. He is right inside Himself. God makes us righteous. He makes us right inside.

Justice and righteousness came when people obeyed the law in the Old Testament. Justice and righteousness comes in Jesus Christ in the New Testament. We who believe in Jesus as Savior and Lord have Christ's righteousness given to us. God judges right in what Christ did for us when He saved us. (See Rom. 3:25.) When Paul lived, some people had the idea that if God forgave sin then God was judging wrong. Some people thought God should not forgive sin.

Paul said God judges right when He made a way for sinful people to be made righteous in Christ. (See Rom. 3:25.) We come to Christ only through faith. We do not come to Christ through good things we do. God gives us the righteousness of Christ as a gift to those who believe in Jesus. (See Rom. 5:17.) People who try to become saved by doing good things are going back to the idea that salvation comes by doing good works and not by grace. (See Rom. 9:30-32.)

Some people who live today may think that justification is too easy. But it was not easy for God. Leon Morris tells how hard it was with this story: A bum breaks into your house and steals something that cost a lot of money and is important to you. You forgive the person later. It may be hard to forgive. If the thief was not a bum but was your best friend, it would be harder to forgive him. If the thief was your best friend, you would feel that your friend broke your trust. It would be harder to forgive your friend. But what if the thief was your son. Think how you would feel. Yes, you would forgive your son. That is what parents would do. But it will not be easy to forgive him. That is somewhat like it is for God to forgive us. We are His children. We did wrong against Him. He still forgives us. His forgiveness is not easy. He forgives us. He also justifies us. He makes us like as if we had never sinned. God justifies us. That is a wonderful work of God—a miracle. That is more than we can fully understand.

Ralph Neighbour has said, "Jesus can never look at me without seeing His own blood. Because I asked Him to forgive me and cleanse me with His blood, no one in heaven can look at me without seeing me through the blood of Jesus Christ."

PERSONAL LEARNING ACTIVITY 5

In chapter 5 the writer uses several words to explain about the atonement. Write a few words to explain what each of the words below mean.

1. Substitution: _____

2. Covenant: _____

3. Sacrifice: _____

4. Redemption: _____

5. Reconciliation: _____

6. Expiation: _____

7. Justification: _____

---

[1]Leon Morris, *The Atonement* (Downers Grove: Inter Varsity Press, 1983), pp. 45-46; paraphrased from regular English copy.

CHAPTER 6

The Doctrine of Salvation

"God loved the world so much that he gave his only
Son, so that everyone who believes in him may not die
but have eternal life."
John 3:16 (GNB)

S in is real in people's lives. Bad things happen when people sin. We can see everywhere what happens because of sin. A person will have bad problems many times because of sin.

David showed the deep need of all people when he asked God to make him clean from sin. (See Ps. 51:7.) Isaiah gave words of hope for sinful people when he said, "You are stained red with sin, but I will wash you as clean as snow. Although your stains are deep red [very bad], you will be as white as wool" (Isa. 1:18, GNB). God has a plan to save people from sin. That plan is finished in Jesus Christ.

The most important thing Jesus does is save people. The name *Jesus* means God saves. Often the Bible says that salvation was the work of Jesus. (See Luke 19:10; 1 Tim. 1:15; Heb. 9:26.) We can be saved only because of God's love. This truth is clear in the best-known Bible verse--John 3:16. That verse tells us that God's love is for the whole world. "God loved the world." Not many verses in the Bible make it clearer than this verse. God's good news is for everyone.

A preacher said this, "God's will to save is as wide as His will to create." God loves all the people in our world today. He loves all different races of people and colors of people. He loves people from every country. God loves all people whether good or

83

bad. God loves the people who are easy to love. He loves the people who are hard to love. God loves the person who worships him. He loves the person who never thinks about Him.

Augustine said, "God loves each one of us as if there was only one of us to love." All Christians who feel the way God feels will really care about people. We will be like missionaries. We will be burdened for the world like God.

We are not good enough for God's love. God gives His love. He gave His only Son. Many people in the history of this world have not accepted God. The stories of history are full of murder, killing, lies, wars, and unfair things. Many people have decided to stay away from God and turn God away. He loved all people even though they are not good enough for His love. God gives salvation to all who will believe in Him. God does this just because He is full of grace. (See Eph. 2:8-10.)

Salvation: Grace Through Faith

Paul made it clear that we are saved by the grace of God. *Grace* is one of the most beautiful words in the Bible. It means think well of (favor), thanks, goodwill, and gratitude [to be thankful for something]. It also has the idea of being good, gentle, and helpful. The deep-down meaning of *grace* is to make a gift. The Greek language word for *grace* is *charis*. This word talks about God's love. His kind of love brings good from bad. It always works to save sinners and to keep those sinners in a good friendship with Him.

The Bible is the story of God's saving grace. The Old Testament shows God's loving-kindness through His friendship with people. God made agreements with His people (covenants). In the New Testament, we find a new covenant in God's gift of Jesus: "God gave the Law through Moses, but grace and truth came through Jesus Christ" (John 1:17, GNB).

Salvation does not come to us because we have faith in Christ and do good things. In Galatians 5:4 (KJV), Paul talked about people who "are fallen from grace." Paul did not mean that someone who was saved became lost. He was saying the people in Galatia had fallen away from teaching salvation by grace. Salvation can only come by God's grace.

Salvation: Steps in the Plan

Conviction. I heard the good news about Jesus the first time when I was 15 years old. I was lost without Jesus. My family was lost without Jesus. I lived in a place that did not believe in God. When I heard about Jesus, I never asked if what I heard was true. I went to a church because I had nothing to do. I heard the pastor preach. The pastor made an invitation after he preached. I walked to the front of the church. I told the pastor that I was lost. I was going to hell. I wanted to accept Jesus for my Savior. I got down on my knees with the pastor. I prayed "the sinner's prayer." I prayed about my sin. I prayed, accepting Jesus. How could a 15-year-old boy who knew nothing about religion, the Bible, or Christ start to understand so fast? It happened because God worked in my heart to show Jesus to me.

I have preached in other countries where people have never heard about Christ. Still, people came to accept Christ when I gave an invitation. People have told me: "I have never heard this before, but there is something in what you said that touches me. I believe it, and I accept Jesus as my Savior." One time I preached to some people in Africa. Some other people were trying to break up the church service while I preached. Those people walked outside the building. They beat drums. They shouted for their gods to hurt the meeting. When I gave the invitation, 35 people who had never heard about Christ before accepted Him as Savior.

The only way people can understand the great truth that Jesus is the Son of God is when God makes it clear for people. Paul wrote, "No one can confess, 'Jesus is Lord,' unless he is guided by the Holy Spirit" (1 Cor. 12:3, GNB). Jesus said, "No one can come to me unless the Father who sent me draws him" (John 6:44, GNB). So when a person says from his heart that Jesus is Lord, that person can only say so because God makes it clear. God has worked in that person's heart to give that person the right understanding.

Repentance. There are many wrong ideas in the world. Sometimes religious leaders teach these wrong ideas. Not long ago I heard a preacher say the New Testament does not teach us what to do about sex. That preacher was wrong. One time I got a letter saying the Bible does not teach that there is a hell. That is a wrong idea. When we have wrong ideas and when we do wrong things, we need to change. *Repentance* means to change. The New Testament word for *repentance* is *metanoia*. This word has three important ideas. It means a change of mind; to have a feeling of sorrow; and to turn away from sin. It means to turn to God.

A person who repents will admit the terrible wrong of sin. Isaiah 1:5-6 (GNB) shows sin clearly: "Why do you keep on rebelling? Do you want to be punished even more? Israel, your head is already covered with wounds, and your heart and mind are sick. From the head to foot there is not a healthy spot on your body. You are covered with bruises and sores and open wounds. Your wounds have not been cleaned or bandaged. No medicine has been put on them."

When a person repents, that person sees that sin has power to take over a person's life. (See John 8:34-44.) I heard a story one time about some men and women who took some heroin. The heroin ruined their bodies. They could not move. Their bodies were paralyzed. That is what sin does. Sin makes us be like we are paralyzed. Sin takes over and ruins everything. People often try to find a way to excuse what they do wrong. Some people say they have the right to live their own lives the way they want. Some people say they have the right to do wrong if it makes them happy. When people think like that, they do not care about the feelings other people have. They do not care what hurts other people. And, it is more important, people do not follow what the Bible clearly teaches. But God's Word never changes. His Word tells us the truth. The Bible says that when we live in a selfish way, we are living in sin. People who do not know God always live in sin of unbelief. People who will not accept God's truth live in sin. Galatians 5:19-21 (GNB) says: "What human nature does is quite plain. It shows itself in immoral, filthy, and indecent actions; in worship of idols and witchcraft. People become enemies and they fight; they become jealous, angry, and ambitious. They separate into parties and groups; they are envious, get drunk, have orgies, and do other things like these. I warn you now as I have before: those who do these things will not possess the Kingdom of God."

Repentance means three things:

1. *It means letting God change your mind.* The only way God can cleanse the sinner and fellowship with the sinner is for the unsaved person to have a big change in his thinking. The sinner must change his mind about right and wrong.

2. *It means letting God change your heart.* To change your heart means to have a change deep inside your life. Our deep feelings must be fully changed and made right. Our deep feelings, not just our thoughts, must be changed. When repentance changes our deep feelings about right and wrong, we will hate sin as God hates sin.

3. *It means letting God change what you do.* When a person is saved, the things that person does will change. The saved person stops doing things that break God's law. That person starts doing right things. The saved person starts living in a way that changes the world around him.

Acceptance. When a person accepts Christ as Savior, he must also accept Him as Lord. Salvation is not only changing from death in hell to life in heaven. The new birth of salvation means starting a whole new life. The person who believes in Jesus starts a new life as soon as that person is saved. You are not *going* to be born again when you go to heaven. You *are* born again. Life is fully new. The new Christian is different inside. He is now going on a new way in life.

A person does not learn a lot and then that person is saved. A person must make a decision to accept Jesus. You can study about Jesus all your life and never really know Him as Savior. Many people in the world teach about religion. Those teachers agree that Jesus was a great leader. Those teachers can talk about the words of Jesus. Some religions that do not follow Christ still accept Jesus as an important religious teacher. But Jesus is more than a great teacher. Jesus made this clear to Nicodemus. Nicodemus was a good man. He was a religious leader. Still, Nicodemus had to be born again. The Ten Commandments and the Golden Rule are good to follow. They cannot save a person.

When little babies are born, they are not already born into the kingdom of God. Human birth and being born again are two different things. Every person is born with a nature that is sinful.

(See Ps. 51:5; Isa. 53:6.) Each person needs to be born again in the spirit. Nicodemus was a nice man. But Jesus said he had to be born again. My father had a hard time understanding salvation. He was a good man. He worked hard to get better. But he could not find salvation. One time I was talking with him at 2:00 a.m. I said: "Dad, you never will become a Christian by working at it like you are trying to do. You will never accept Jesus by trying to get your life straight." Then it happened. My Dad began to see the truth of salvation. In the past he could not see the spiritual truth. Now he began to see. He prayed, "God, forgive me and save me." Salvation came to my dad at that moment when he accepted Him. When Dad accepted Christ and let Christ do the saving, Dad was saved.

A good way to remember what we have said about salvation is to use the word FAITH: Forsaking All, I Trust Him. Jesus made it clear that He knew the way of salvation. It does not matter what anyone else thinks about salvation. It does not matter what anyone else wishes about salvation. Christ made the way of salvation. Christ is the one who can tell us how to be saved. For that reason, we must give up our ideas and give up to Christ.

Confession. Sometimes we hear about people who are secret believers. These are people who believe Jesus is the Son of God. These are people who accept Jesus as Savior. But these people do not want anyone to know they have accepted Jesus. Maybe they are afraid someone will make fun of them. Maybe they are afraid someone will hurt them because they became a Christian. You and I cannot judge if a person has real faith in Him or not. But Jesus taught clearly that we must not be ashamed of Jesus. We must tell openly about Him. That is what it means to confess Jesus openly. (See Matt. 10:32-33.) Salvation is not just believing a few things in your mind. Salvation is giving your whole life to Jesus so that He is your Lord.

Faith in Christ means that we are ready to openly confess Jesus as our Savior. If you have faith that Jesus will save you, you are ready for Jesus to be the most important thing in your whole life. No person can be saved if that person lets houses or family or land be more important than Jesus in his life. (See Matt. 19:29.) *Faith* means to trust Him and to obey Him. *Faith* means we do not stay quiet about Jesus. We are ready to stand up for Him. *Faith* means we will openly confess Him. Can a person be saved if that person does not follow Jesus? How can a person get the wonderful gift of salvation but not be ready to follow Jesus? How can a true believer keep quiet about his faith in Christ? How can a person believe that living forever is more important than living on earth and then that person be too afraid to stand up for Christ?

It seems that Matthew 10:32-33 is showing how a person who believes in Jesus should live. New believers in Jesus must learn and grow a lot. New Christians will make mistakes. Remember that even Peter denied Jesus. But it is not possible to think that when a person first accepts Jesus that person could hold in his heart a plan to stay quiet about salvation.

In Southern Baptist churches, the invitation time is planned to give a chance for the new believer in Jesus to confess to all the people that he has accepted Christ. Most of the time new believers in Jesus are baptized soon after they openly confess Him. That is because baptism is also openly showing the new believer's faith. This is the way the Christian life begins and continues. The New Christian will continue to openly tell about salvation in Christ.

The church needs to help the new Christian. In every church there is a need for Christians to know how to help new Christians. When a person first accepts Jesus, Christians who know how to help the new Christian need to explain salvation clearly. The new Christian needs answers for all his questions. The new Christian needs a copy of the Bible to read. The new Christian needs things to read that will help with doubt about salvation.

The *Personal Commitment Guide* is a good example of a little book that can help the new Christian. Satan is always fast to try to hurt the new Christian with doubt about salvation. Satan is fast to try to tempt the new Christian. We must do all we can to give the new Christian the armor of God and the sword of the Word. We must help the new Christian against Satan. We must help the new Christian with the Bible.

Salvation: the Nature of Saving Faith
If a person wants to be saved, that person must have faith. Faith

for salvation is not just thinking that life is good. Faith for salvation is not just agreeing with some beliefs. Faith for salvation comes from your mind, your deep feelings (emotions), and your deep wants (will).

Saving faith comes from your mind (is intellectual). Faith for salvation is not faith that does not think about things. We know what God has done. We know about the life of Christ. Those things were written down. Some things written in the Bible are hard to understand. Some people will not believe in Jesus because of His miracles. His being born to a woman who never had sex, His resurrection from the dead, and His death on the cross are hard things to understand. Faith for salvation decides to accept these things that are important for salvation even though they are hard to understand.

Some people ask, What must a person know before he can be saved? This is not easy to answer. A person is saved when he puts his faith in Jesus Christ. After a person is saved, that person must learn many important things. For us to learn more about our Christian faith is good. There are three things a person must know and believe to be saved: (1) Jesus really did live here on earth as a real person. (See 1 John 1:1-3; 4:2-3.) (2) One must accept Jesus on this level—Jesus Christ is the Son of God. (3) Jesus is the way to salvation. (See Acts 4:12.)

Saving faith is emotional. All people are different. Some people become saved. They have many strong feelings. Some people do not feel much. Everyone does have feelings. Emotions are deep feelings we have inside. Everyone has emotions. When a person is saved, the whole person is saved. Emotions are part of the experience of salvation. We will have deep feelings about salvation because God forgave our sins and gave us new life. When we become saved, big changes happen in our lives. Some people may cry when they are saved. Some people may not cry. But the salvation experience always touches deep in our souls. Deep feelings do not make salvation happen. It does not matter how deep the feeling is. The feeling does not bring salvation or prove salvation.

Saving faith is volitional. Volition means what I want. When I say saving faith is volitional, I mean a person must decide he wants to be saved. Today people have a hard time understanding the word *faith*. The reason people have a hard time is that the word can have different meanings. Sometimes it means believing some facts. Sometimes people speak about faith to mean the name of their church group. Sometimes the word is used to mean some unclear spiritual feeling. In the Bible the word *faith* always has as part of its meaning a deep, strong decision that the person makes. Christ said we need to see that believing in Him might make life hard for us. When we believe in Jesus, we need to make a deep-down decision about it. (See Luke 14:25-33.)

Paul is a good example for us. When he became a Christian, life was hard for him. He knew life as a Christian would be hard before he decided to accept Jesus. Paul accepted Jesus anyway. (See Phil. 3:7-9.)

Even after we become Christians, we are still people. We still have sin in us. We never give our lives all the way to Christ. As new Christians grow in Jesus, they find places in their lives they have not yet given to Jesus. This really does happen. When a person first accepts Jesus as Savior, that person must not think about keeping any part of his life back from Christ. Each person at the time of salvation must decide to give his whole life to Christ.

Salvation: What It Means to Believers

When a person becomes saved, every part of the person is touched and changed by salvation. God's saving power reaches every part of a person. Salvation brings forgiveness from sin, joy, and peace. It brings a new life in Christ. We need to say several important things that will help explain what salvation means to people who believe in Jesus.

Salvation happens in three times. Salvation must be explained as happening in three times. First, a person believes in Jesus. He is saved at the moment of decision for Christ. Second, the Christian grows in Christ. He learns how to follow Jesus. Third, the Christian will end salvation in heaven. Baptists often talk about these three times of salvation this way: I *am* saved. I am *being* saved. I *will* be saved.

The first words mean a person needs to decide for Christ. The second words mean a Christian grows in Christ. This is what Philippians 2:12 means when it talks about working out our own salvation. This does not mean we work to be saved. This means that salvation changes us. Every day by the power of the Holy Spirit the salvation experience is changing us more. The third words mean that some day we will meet Christ in heaven. Our salvation will be full at that time.

Salvation means that God calls us. Many years ago Baptists did not agree about the idea of predestination. *Predestination* is the idea that God decides before it happens what will happen in each person's life. Baptists had strong disagreements about this idea. John Calvin was the man who wrote long ago about predestination. What he wrote is what the Baptists argued about. Some people believe in strong predestination. This idea is that God decided some people will be saved and some people will not be saved. Many people who have this idea do not like missions work. They say that missions work goes against God's control. Not many people still have this old idea today. Now we can look at the idea of predestination in a better way.

The idea of *election* is a belief that talks about the work of God in salvation. Words like *predestined, called, chosen, elect,* and *foreknowledge* are words used in the Bible to talk about God's work in salvation. (See Mark 13:20; John 13:18; Rom. 8:29-30; Eph. 1:4; 1 Thess. 2:12; 2 Thess. 2:13; 1 Pet. 1:1-2.) These words in their verses in the Bible seem to mean that God chose Israel to be His people. That is what God meant to say. God chose Israel, no matter that Israel was not good enough for God. God chooses believers, the new Israel, no matter that believers are not good enough for God.

We can argue about predestination and miss an important point. God started the work of salvation. He chose and called each believer. God wants to give salvation to everyone. He calls to every person in the world. When we talk about Jesus, people will accept Jesus for their savior. When we do not talk about Jesus, only a few people will accept Jesus for their savior. So we have a responsibility to share the call of God with the world.

God calls to everyone in the world. Does that make His call less important? If all people are called, is my call still special? To help answer that question, you might talk to people about their salvation experience. People will tell you how God worked through different things and different experiences. As God worked on them, they came to the time when they accepted Christ. Each believer might argue about election when he is talking about ideas. Few people will argue against election in his own experience. All of us feel that God works on us one by one to lead us to our own salvation decision.

When God saves us, He has a reason. The verses listed above have words like this: "Be holy and without fault" (Eph. 1:4, GNB). "Be conformed to the likeness of his Son" (Rom. 8:29). "Live the kind of life that pleases God" (1 Thess. 2:12). God chose us, and that is wonderful! One reason why that is wonderful is because God wants to use us in His work of saving the world. We are called into a new Kingdom. We are called from this world. We now have a different relationship with God and with people. Now we have a new job from God for us to do. We have a new mission.

The apostle Paul had a deep feeling God was leading his life. Paul believed Jesus saved him for a good reason. Paul wanted to do everything God wanted for him to do when God saved him on the road to Damascus. When Jesus saved Paul, Jesus broke the hold the past had on Paul. Jesus broke the hold of sin and guilt. Jesus gave Paul a new responsibility for a new life of service. We, too, are called by God to serve Him. We must never forget God called us to be like Jesus in the way we live and in the way we serve other people.

Salvation means adoption. A few different words are used in the New Testament to explain the new relationship the Christian has with God. We can have this relationship because of Jesus' blood. *Adoption* is one of these words. This word helps us understand salvation. *Adoption* also helps us understand the real relationship we have with God because of Christ. We are now sons and daughters of God. (See Rom. 8:15-17; Gal. 4:1-7).

We can see this new relationship in the Model Prayer. Jesus taught us to speak to God as Father. This was a new idea for the Jews. The Jews would not even say God's name. They would not call Him Father. We can find where God is called Father sometimes in the Old Testament. When God is called Father in the Old Testament, the idea is that He is Father of Israel. *Father* is not used in the Old Testament to talk about one person's relationship with God. We find something different in the New Testament. Now, because of what Jesus did, we can call God *Father*. Jesus used the word *Abba* to talk about God. This word is a family word like *Daddy*. This is a close and loving word for God.

God adopted us as His children. The New Testament shows clearly what happens now that we are God's children. (See Rom. 8:15-17.) We share all Jesus has gotten from the Father now that we are adopted sons and daughters. Now we share in Christ's glory. This is part of what our salvation means. We are sons and daughters of God. God relates to us as His own children. He teaches us. He leads us. He helps us change. He uses us. He blesses us. He helps us. He corrects us. As our Heavenly Father, He is happy or hurt by what we do.

Salvation means joined with Christ. Some other words that show what happens to us when God saves us are *union with Christ.* John 14:20 (GNB) tells a great true thing. "When that day comes, you will know that I am in my Father and that you are in me, just as I am in you." Many times Paul said that believers are in Christ. (See Rom. 6:11; 8:1; 2 Cor. 5:17; Gal. 3:27; Eph. 2:10.)

Jesus said that our union with God is like a vine joined with its branches. We can read Jesus' words in John 15:1-8. We are joined with Christ. His life flows through us. We get from Him what we need to live spiritually. We start to have Christian fruit in our lives like the kind of fruit Jesus made.

Another way to say that same idea is that we start to live the way He would live. Because we are joined with Christ, everything in the believer's life is touched. We become part of the living body of Christ. In Galatians 2:19-20 (GNB) Paul showed what happens because we are joined with Christ: "I have been put to death with Christ . . . so that it is no longer I who live, but it is Christ who lives in me. This life that I live now, I live by faith in the Son of God, who loved me and gave his life for me." These verses really show the Christian is spiritually joined with the risen Christ. Because we are joined with Him, we have strength with no end to do God's work. God's power can heal, save, clean from sin, and forgive. His power flows from the risen Christ into the hearts of His real followers.

Salvation: Saved and Secure

Sometimes you might see the words *eternal security* or *security of the believer.* These words mean the same thing. They mean that when a person is saved, he is always saved. He will never be lost and without Jesus again. This does not mean that anyone who joins a church is *secure* or saved. This idea of *eternal security* comes from what the Bible says about salvation.

I preached my first revival in East Tennessee. East Tennessee is where I grew up. Several times I asked if someone was saved or not. The answer was, "He professed the Lord" or "She professed the Lord." This meant that the person had said he was saved. Then I asked if that person was going to church, living for the Lord, and serving Him. The answer was, "No, but he professed the Lord." I heard that answer several times. I started to wonder about that word *professed.* I started to see that this word did not mean much. Hebrews 4:14 (GNB) tells us with strong words to "hold firmly to the faith we profess." *Hold firmly* means to hold without ever letting go. It means to hold on like a bulldog.

When a person truly accepts Christ as Savior, God gives that person a promise that he will never be lost. (See John 3:36; 10:27-29; Phil. 1:5-6; 1 Pet. 1:5.) Other verses with strong words tell the believer he must not think lightly about his salvation. We will see these verses later. We can see that the truth about eternal security can make us feel good. I am not saved because I am always strong. I am saved because God is always strong. If we were saved because we always stay strong, not many people would be saved in the end.

When God makes us secure about salvation, He does not take away from us our freedom to choose. E. Y. Mullins was talking about this idea when he said that God does not build walls so much as he builds wills.

When a person is really saved, that experience changes all of life. The person who really feels God's free grace will stay faithful to God for all of life. The person who really gives his life to Jesus Christ will stay faithful to God for all of life. Believers are still weak. They will fail sometimes. God does not like it when we do wrong and do not repent. The true believer will know and feel this. The true believer, deep in his heart, will always want to do the things God says are right. The true believer will always want to have fellowship with God.

Baptists do not accept the idea of falling from grace. We do not accept this idea. This idea does not see that God has the power to hold and keep His children. Baptists also do not accept the idea that if a person is saved, then He can live in a bad way if he wants. This idea is not right. It does not see the great change that salvation makes in a person's life.

If we want to understand *eternal security* right, we must understand salvation the way the Bible teaches it. God gives us salvation because of His grace. When a person is saved, that person has forgiveness of sin and a new life in fellowship with God. The believer will never lose that salvation. Because of His grace, God gives us salvation. God lets us stay saved. God will take us to heaven. We are in God's hand. His hand is strong.

PERSONAL LEARNING ACTIVITY 6

On the lines below, write the story of your salvation. Finish writing each sentence.

1. Before I met Christ, I _____

_____

2. I became saved when I _____

_____

3. Now that God has saved me, I will _____

_____

CHAPTER 7

The Christian Life: Priests of God

Come as living stones, and let yourselves be used in
building the spiritual temple, where you will serve as
holy priests to offer spiritual and acceptable sacrifices to
God through Jesus Christ. . . . You are the chosen
race, the King's priests, the holy nation, God's own
people, chosen to proclaim the wonderful acts of God,
who called you out of darkness into his own marvelous
light.
1 Peter 2:5,9 (GNB)

I t is an important time when a baby is born in a family. Many changes happen when the new baby comes home. Mother, father, brothers, and sisters give the new baby a lot of time and care. The whole family must make plans around the needs of the baby. The family must feed the baby, change the baby's diapers, love the baby, and care for all the needs of the baby. Everyone knows that this little new baby cannot take care of himself. The family must do everything for the baby for several months. The baby starts to grow and learn. It will be a long time before the baby grows up and can take care of himself. Everyone knows the baby will grow up. The goal of life is to grow.

The newborn Christian must also grow. When a person is saved (born again), the person has a new life. It is a birth, the beginning of a new life. The new Christian is like a baby. The goal for every newborn Christian is to grow up and become a full-grown Christian (mature). Each new Christian needs to grow up and become a right-living follower of Jesus. Growing up in Christ is the Christian life.

The Bible says many things about Christian life. Christians have privileges. Christians also get to do special things. Christians have special things they must do (responsibilities). Christians are God's priests. Because Christians are God's priests, they have special work to do. We need to look in the Bible to find the right way to grow in the Christian life.

The Christian Life: Priests and Temples of God

When Christianity first began, it did not have many people earning money as Christian workers. Christianity was led by people working for free. We call people like that *laymen*. *Laymen* led the churches, and all the members were just laypeople. All believers were equal in the church, and all believers used their gifts from God's Spirit. Later the church began to see two different groups of people—the clergy and the laity. *Clergy* means the people who were paid ministers for the church. These were pastors and other workers. *Laity* means members of the church who do not earn money from the church. Early after Jesus' time, the church started to make these two groups. Soon the paid workers (ministers) thought they were more important than regular members. Regular members soon just watched the paid workers do all the work. The regular members did not do much in the churches.

The idea to divide the church people into two groups like this is not in the Bible. The Bible says that to God all Christians are equal. You can read the Book of Acts or you could read verses like Ephesians 4:11-13. In those places you will see that every Christian is to work for the Lord. Every Christian must be a minister. The New Testament teaches that all believers are priests for God. All of God's priests are to work for Him. We can see three important ideas about the priesthood of believers: (1) All believers are equal before God. (2) Each person has the right to go straight to the Father and not through some other person. (3) Each believer has different gifts from the Holy Spirit. Each believer must use his gifts to work for the Lord. This is what we believe. This is our doctrine. This idea was forgotten for a long time after Jesus' time. About 400 years ago, the church remembered this doctrine again. This happened during the Protestant Reformation. But the idea was not fully thought through at that time.

Baptists have always known that the idea of the priesthood of believers is important. From the start of the Baptists, we have said that every person has the right to go straight to God without going through a priest. Every believer is responsible to work for the Lord by helping other people. This is our history. This idea has been important in our history. It has touched every part of Baptist life.

After World War II, people started thinking again about the responsibility of the regular church member. Many people in different church groups wrote about how regular church members had responsibility for working for the Lord. Regular church members must do more than just hand out the church programs and pass the offering plates on Sunday morning.

We know that God calls all believers to work for Him. The regular church member cannot pay someone else to take care of his need to work for the Lord. Each person must someday explain to the Lord how he used the spiritual gifts God gave him. No one can say to God that he paid someone else to do his responsibility to serve the Lord.

Two important verses that explain about the priesthood of believers are 1 Peter 2:9-10 (GNB): "You are the chosen race, the King's priests, the holy nation, God's own people, chosen to proclaim the wonderful acts of God, who called you out of darkness into his own marvelous light. At one time you were not God's people, but now you are his people; at one time you did not know God's mercy, but now you have received his mercy." These verses give a clear idea about the people of God.

Peter used ideas from the Old Testament to show what Christians were like. Peter said Christians are a chosen people. God chose people who are Christians. God chose the Jews to tell people who were not Jews (Gentiles) about God. In the same way, God chose the church to work for Him. A Christian is part of the King's priests. Christians can go straight to God with prayers. God has called Christians to be a "holy nation." Christians are like a nation of people who will serve God. Paul talked about Christians as "a pure people who belong to him [God]" (Titus 2:14). Christians really do belong to God. Christians must do what God wants and must do God's work.

These words are all in the Old Testament. In the New Testament, the full meaning of the words is made clear. When Baptists first started as a church group, they strongly believed that every Christian is a priest and is equal to all other Christians. This belief has helped us understand all our beliefs in new ways. This belief has helped us know how to do the work of the church. The doctrine of the priesthood of the believer has helped us make our churches in our hometowns. It has helped us make our whole Southern Baptist Convention.

You can find a full explanation of this doctrine in the book *The Doctrine of the Priesthood of the Believers* by Walter B. Shurden. Every person who accepts Christ as Savior gets from God all the blessings Jesus gets from God. Every believer is fully equal with all other believers. The New Testament uses the words *priests* and *priesthood* to show this idea about Christians are equal. Now we are brothers of Jesus, and we are a part of His kingdom. (See Rev. 1:6; 5:10.)

Now we are priests. We show God to other people. Each of us is like a bridge builder between God and other people. We help bring people across the bridge to God when we witness in His name. Now we are priests. We can give our own lives to God as a sacrifice when we witness. Also, we do this when we give praise to God. We give our lives to God when we pray for others. We give our lives to God when we help other people or when we visit other people. Now we are priests. We can go straight to God without getting anyone else to help us. Only Jesus brings us to God, not some other person. We can go to God because of what God has done for us through His Son. The Book of Hebrews talks about our rights as Christians. We can be brave before God's throne of grace. (See Heb. 4:16.)

In Romans 12:1, we see some words that are hard to change from Greek to English. We see these words *spiritual worship*. *Latreian* is the Greek language word that is said in English by the word *worship*. This word means a priest doing religious things.

We know there is no more sacrifice in the Temple. All believers are priests. We work as priests by giving ourselves to work for Christ. We could say that we lay our bodies on the altar. We give our lives to God and His work.

There are many verses in the New Testament that use ideas from the Jewish sacrifices. Many of these verses are talking about all believers becoming priests for God. We see that this is a big idea in the New Testament. Often the New Testament says Christians are a temple. These verses are saying the same thing as the verses that call Christians "priests." The New Testament calls Christians *temples* in three different ways. (1) Each believer is a temple. (See 1 Cor. 6:19.) (2) A local church is a temple. (See 1 Cor. 3:16-17.) (3) All God's people together are called a temple. (See Eph. 2:21.)

The Greek language word for the whole Jewish temple is *hieron*. In the big Jewish Temple was the small holy of holies place where God met the priest. The Greek language word for the holy of holies is *naos.* The New Testament in the Greek language says that Christians are temples. The Greek language word *naos* is always used about Christians. The Greek language word *hieron* is never used to talk about Christians. Christians are the holy of holies place kind of temple.

In Matthew 27:51, the Bible says that the veil in the Jewish Temple was torn from top to bottom. Ephesians 2:14 says that the wall that used to separate was torn down. This is great because this means that now all who believe have full and free entry to God. This also means that now God lives in the life of each believer. You and I are God's *naos.* Now the local church is God's *naos.* All the people of God are God's *naos.* God lives in His people. He lives in each one of His people. God lives in us, but often we do not live like it. God saved us so He could live in us. God lives in us. That is what priesthood of believers means. Now we must live for God because He lives in us.

Paul was talking about this truth when he said believers are "living stones" being built by God into a "spiritual temple." (See 1 Pet. 2:5.) Paul used an idea almost like this one in Ephesians 2:19-22. The old Temple in Jerusalem was made from huge stones. Each stone is made just the right size to fit.

Josephus wrote about the history of the Temple. He wrote that Herod, the man who paid to build the Temple, did not let the workers use hammers to cut the stones in the Temple area. Every stone was cut just right at the place where the stone was dug from the ground. Each stone was cut perfect. That is what Christ wants to do with us. Each of us has a place in the spiritual house Christ is building. We must give our lives fully to Him. We must be priests to God as He says. We must let Christ change us until we fit His plan perfectly.

The Christian Life: Sanctification and Growth
First Peter 1:14 says believers are obedient children. We are never to stay as babies, but we do not miss a time of childhood as we grow in the Lord. First Peter 1:14-15 (GNB) tells what *obedience* means: "Do not allow your lives to be shaped by these desires you had when you were still ignorant. Instead, be holy in all that you do, just as God who called you is holy."

Sanctification is the word the Bible uses to explain how Christians grow in Christ. The word means to be set apart or to be holy. Like the word *salvation*, this word has three time ideas. (1) We are sanctified (set apart) when we are first saved. So every believer is a saint. (2) If we are growing in Christ, then we are always being sanctified (being made holy). (3) We will be fully sanctified (will be made holy) when we meet Christ in heaven. Baptists do not believe that anyone is perfectly sinless (full sanctification) in this life. We have the goal to be perfect, but no one is perfect yet.

Matthew 6:33 says, "Instead, be concerned above everything else with the Kingdom of God and with what he requires of you, and he will provide you with all these other things." (GNB) Jesus has a plan for the way we live our lives. There are many things that seem important in life. We need to study the Bible and learn how to know what is most important in life. Life is more important than things we have. (See Luke 12:15.) It is important that we stay strong in the power of God. (See Eph. 6:10.) It is important that we remember that we must explain to God why we live the way we do live. (See Rom. 14:12.)

Charles Sheldon wrote a book called *In His Steps*. This book really touched my life. I thought a lot about the idea of that question in the book, What would Jesus do? That question helped me try to follow His example.

In Philippians 3:10-12 (GNB), we can clearly see the goal of Christian living: "All I want is to know Christ and to experience the power of his resurrection, to share in his sufferings and become like him in his death, in the hope that I myself will be raised from death to life. I do not claim that I have already succeeded or have already become perfect. I keep striving to win the prize for which Christ Jesus has already won me to himself." In these verses, Paul showed the best reason for growing in Christ. You might think that after so many years of serving Christ that Paul would already understand Jesus and the Christian life. But Paul knew that growing in Christ never stops. There is much more to learn and to grow.

To know some about a person and to know a person well is different. To know some about a person is good. But when you know a person well, that is better. The word *know* has the idea in it of knowing a person because of good personal experience. The *Good News Bible* tries to explain verse 12 like this, "I keep striving to win the prize for which Christ Jesus has already won me to himself." To know Christ means that we understand what God wants us to do in His plan for the world. Paul wanted to do everything God was planning for Paul to do when God saved Paul.

Paul said clearly that he was not yet fully grown up in Christ. The *Good News Bible* uses the word *perfect* in verse 12. This verse is more clear if the words *full grown* or *mature* are used instead of *perfect*. See the strong words Paul used in verses 13-14: "Brothers, I really do not think I have already won it; the one thing I do, however, is to forget what is behind me and do my best to reach what is ahead. So I run straight toward the goal in order to win the prize, which is God's call through Christ Jesus to the life above." Paul really wanted to grow in Christ. Paul was working hard to do God's work. He did not want Jesus to feel hurt if Paul should fail to do God's work. Paul was like a runner in a race. Paul was going to the finish line, trying as hard as he could to reach the goal.

Ephesians 1:15-20 (GNB) has a beautiful prayer that Paul said for the Christians in Ephesus:

For this reason, ever since I heard about your faith in the Lord Jesus and your love for all of God's people, I have not stopped giving thanks for you. I remember you in my prayers and ask the God of our Lord Jesus Christ, the glorious Father, to give you the Spirit, who will make you wise and will reveal God to you, so that you will know him. I ask that your minds may be opened to see his light, so that you will know what is the hope to which he has called you, how rich are the wonderful blessings he promises his people, and how very great is his power at work in us who believe. This power working in us is the same as the mighty strength which he used when he raised Christ from death and seated him at his right hand in the heavenly world.

This prayer has some important ideas for all believers. First, Paul prayed that the Ephesian Christians have "the Spirit, who will make you wise and reveal God" (v. 17). The Greek language word for *wisdom* is *sophia.* This word means the good, useful understanding God gives to us. In this verse it has the idea of understanding what God shows us about Himself.

Paul then prayed that your minds may be opened to see his light (v. 18, GNB). When the Bible talks about *heart*, it means the deep inner being. The verse talks about the heart having eyes. This shows the idea that people need more than just a brain that understands things. People need to understand spiritual things deep inside their being. Only the Spirit can understand the deep things of God. Paul wanted the Ephesian people to "know what is the hope to which he has called you, how rich are his wonderful blessings he promises his people, and how very great is his power at work in us who believe" (vv. 18-19, GNB).

Paul did not explain what he meant by "the hope to which he has called you." The idea seems to mean all of what God has for us. *Inheritance* means the great wonderful gifts that God has to give to all of His people. The great power talked about in verse 19 is the power of God that raised Jesus from the dead and raised Jesus to glory in heaven. (See v. 20.)

The Greek language word for *power* in this verse is *dunamis.* This word means power, might, strength, and force. Our English word *dynamite* comes from this Greek word. It is a real surprise that this power from God is ready for all of "us who believe" (v. 19).

God has given us all this for a reason. The reason is so we can live the way God wants us to live. In verse 17, we see the words that say the clear goal for Christian living: "so that you may know him."

The Christian Life: the Call to Continue Growth
The Book of Hebrews warns us about what can happen if we do not grow up in Christ. Hebrews 3:13 (GNB) tells us to "help one another every day." We will help one another grow in Christ if we do that. The Christian must always be careful about how he relates to God.

We will not lose our salvation if we are true believers. But we can miss what God wants for us, and that is bad. We might be like the children of Israel if we are not careful. They were free from Egypt, but they were wandering in the desert. (See Heb. 3:8-9,15.) These verses look back to the time when the Israelites stopped following the Lord at Meribah (Ex. 17:1-7). This place showed forever where the Hebrews rebelled against God.

Just a short time after leaving Sinai, the Israelites had a chance to get the Promised Land. They sent spies into the land to check the land. But the spies became afraid. The people did not trust God. They suffered in the wilderness for 40 years because of that. They stayed in the wilderness until all the older people who had not believed God died. Only Caleb and Joshua, who did trust God, did not die in those 40 years. Because the people did not believe, they did not get to follow what God wanted. (See Deut. 1:26-36.)

Hebrews 3:14 tells us to hold tight to the faith we had when we first walked with Jesus. This verse wants us to get again the joy of our salvation.

Hebrews 5:11--6:3 tells us we need to grow in Christ. The person who wrote the Book of Hebrews wrote about people who were "slow to understand" (v. 11). These were people who did not grow in Christ. They needed easy ideas about God (milk). They were not ready for the hard ideas about God (solid food)

(v. 12). These people were still like babies in Christ (v. 13). These people did not use their minds or their hearts. Some of these believers had been Christians a long time. They should have been ready to teach other people, but they were not.

Christians today who do not read the Bible, study, pray, and help other people are not growing in Christ. They always study again and again the simple things about God. They are not using what they learn, and so they lose what they learn. Sanctification does not happen because you are getting old. Sanctification happens because you give up worldly desires and study and pray and serve and give to the Lord. Paul tried to help the Christians in Corinth understand this. (See 1 Cor. 3:2.) Hebrews 6:1-2 tells us it is important to grow in Christ. If we want to use well what God has given us, we must understand what the Bible teaches.

When a believer does not grow in Christ, he might find his faith is always getting weaker. "Be careful" (Heb. 3:12) could be written, "Look out." The verse tells believers to be careful not to have bad, unbelieving hearts. *Turn away from* is the Greek word *aphistemi.* Our English word *apostasy* comes from that Greek word. That word now means losing your faith. When Jesus lived, that word had the idea of going away from your faith. The readers had to be careful. They were having hard times. Other people were hurting them because they were Christians. They must be careful or they might start having weak faith. If they had weak faith, they might start to rebel against God or step away from God.

The Book of Hebrews also warns the people about backsliding. (See Heb. 6:4-10.) In verse 4, the word *enlightened* (KJV) means to get light. In this verse, it has the idea of people who move from darkness into light. If this verse taught that we can lose our salvation, then it would teach that when a person fell from grace once, he never again could be saved.

Many times I talk with Christians with bad problems. Sometimes their families are torn apart. The husband or wife or son or daughter may not be living a sexually clean life. Many of these people are Christians who are living outside of what God wants for them. Often these people live as if they do not have to answer to God about how they live. Some of these people have lives filled with problems because they rebel against God and family.

The words *fall away* (v. 6, KJV) come from the Greek language word *parapesontas.* This word means to fall aside or to stand aside from. A. T. Robertson was a man who taught the Greek language. He said in *Word Pictures in the New Testament* (volume 5, p. 375), that this word must have a strong meaning. The Greek words in this verse say clearly that if someone falls away it is not possible for that person to come back. This is a hard verse to understand. We can only understand it when we remember all the things the Book of Hebrews says. The writer talked a lot about our sure salvation. Salvation is sure because Christ gave us salvation. Christ still is living and talking with God for us.

It is also important that we understand what was happening in history when the Book of Hebrews was written. It was written in a time when Christians were punished just because they were Christians. If a Christian would deny Christ, then he was not killed. The idea in the verse is that the Christians who denied Christ were crucifying Him again. They were joining in with the people who denied Christ and crucified Him. Those Christians who denied Christ were joining with the people who were enemies to Christ.

The people who were not faithful to Christ could not stay in the church. They showed Jesus was not their Lord. Hebrews 6:9-12 clearly shows that the writer knew his readers were saved. Verses 4-6 can only be understood when we read all the verses.

We are denying Christ when we backslide. That is shown in the verses. We are backsliding if our lives and words deny God's wonderful grace that Christ brought in our lives. The writer of the Book of Hebrews made a list of blessings and understandings that come from faith: we understand (enlightenment); we taste the gifts from heaven; we share in the power of the Holy Spirit and the Holy Spirit is with us; we taste that God's Word is good; and we start to see that the future in heaven will be wonderful. If a person is not faithful to Christ after having all these blessings, then that is a bad sin. Every believer must understand how bad is the guilt of such a sin.

In these verses in Hebrews, the writer tells us we might not be good enough to serve the Lord. The writer says God might not be able to use us in His kingdom. Paul wrote about this same problem in 1 Corinthians 9:24-27. Paul looked at the Christian life like a person who runs in a race. Paul meant the same thing that other verses in the Bible mean: A good test to see whether a person is saved is does he keep going, living for God. The verses in Hebrews say the same thing in a different way. They say the Christian who stops following the Lord is going to have bad troubles. That Christian must give his life fully to Christ. This writer knew the readers would not fall away. (See Heb. 6:9; 10:38-39.) They were firm in Christ Himself. (See Heb. 6:17-20.) He warned them not to take their salvation lightly.

Hebrews 6:7-8 shows the difference between land that makes a good crop and land that only grows thorns. If a Christian does not obey the Lord, then his life shows to the world a useless field full of thorns. This is the wrong way for a Christian to live.

A man was arrested by Hitler. The man's body was beaten, and he was almost killed. The bad men who were beating him could not break his spirit. Finally the army sent the man to a prison where he lived in a terrible place. Later the good army set him free. When the man came out of the prison, his hands, arms, and feet were hurt very bad. But he never did give up. His spirit was never broken. A few months after he got out of prison, he learned that his own son had turned him in to the German police (Gestapo). The man died of a broken spirit about two weeks later. Pain and a hard life in prison did not kill the man. The man died because his son betrayed him. That broke his spirit and led to his death. It is true that our Lord Jesus Christ is hurt before the world and is crucified again by Christians who are not faithful.

PERSONAL LEARNING ACTIVITY 7

All Christians are priests of God. We have some rights and some responsibilities as priests of God. List some rights and responsibilities.

Rights of Priesthood	Responsibilities of Priesthood

CHAPTER 8

The Christian Life: Living in the Spirit

I will ask the Father, and he will give you another Helper, who will stay with you forever. He is the Spirit, who reveals the truth about God. The world cannot receive him, because it cannot see him or know him. But you know him, because he remains you and is in you.
John 14:16-17 (GNB)

T he person who believes in Christ is joined with Christ. The Holy Spirit is the one who joins the believer and Christ. Many Christians do not know all they have in Christ. Think about a story like this: A woman lived in a poor house that was comfortable but small. Then imagine that she found that the house was on land that was full of gold. The gold was there all the time—just below the ground. The woman was rich all the years she lived there. She did not know about her riches. This story can give us an idea about the way many Christians live. Christians have God's Spirit. We are rich, but many of us do not know our riches.

Every person who believes in Christ receives the Holy Spirit the moment he is saved. (See John 14:16-17; 1 Cor. 3:16; 6:19; 1 John 2:27.) Many people who believe in Christ do not know the Spirit is with them. Maybe they did not learn this truth. Maybe they did not listen to what people taught them from the Bible. When some people learn about the Spirit's power in their lives, they wonder why they never heard that teaching before. What we teach about the Holy Spirit is important. This has always been part of Baptist teaching. We will look closely at this important doctrine. We will find the great riches that are ours through the Spirit.

The Person of the Holy Spirit

The Holy Spirit is a Person, not an *It*. The New Testament talks about the Spirit with the word *He*. The New Testament shows the Spirit has personality. The New Testament often says the Holy Spirit is the Spirit of Christ. When we read Paul's writing, we find the same words talking about both Jesus and the Spirit: "Now, the Lord . . . is the Spirit; and where the Spirit of the Lord is present, there is freedom" (2 Cor. 3:17, GNB); "You are his sons. God sent the Spirit of his Son into our hearts" (Gal. 4:6, GNB).

We can see there is a relationship between Christ and the Spirit. We must also see that Christ and the Spirit are not exactly the same in every way. The Spirit is a separate person from Christ. W. H. Griffith Thomas tried to explain the Spirit and Christ like this: "Christ and the Spirit are different yet the same, the same yet different. Perhaps the best expression we can give is [way we can say this is] that while their Personalities are never identical [exactly the same in every way], their presence always is."[1]

Jesus explained the work of the Spirit. Jesus said that the Holy Spirit gives glory to Christ: "The Helper [Holy Spirit] will come, . . . and he will speak about me" (John 15:26, GNB). "He will not speak on his own authority, but he will speak of what he hears. . . . He will give me glory" (John 16:13-14, GNB). This explains why we know so much more about Jesus than we know about the Holy Spirit. Jesus tells us that the Spirit will come. In the Bible, we read about things the Spirit does. But what we learn from the Spirit is about Christ.

We pray to the Father and Son when we pray. We worship Father and Son. We do not pray to the Spirit. We do not worship the Spirit. The Holy Spirit helps us pray, worship, and give glory to Jesus. We do need to be careful when we think about the Spirit. We should not think the Spirit is simply Jesus in a spirit form. That is not right thinking.

The Work of the Holy Spirit

What is the work of the Holy Spirit? What does the Spirit do in the life of the church? What does the Spirit do in the everyday lives of people? There are many parts to the answer. We will now look at some of the parts of the answer. The answers we will see are true. We have seen some of these true answers already. We will only talk a little about the true things we have already seen. We will talk more fully about some new things.

The Holy Spirit inspired the biblical writers. (See chap. 1.) The Bible is the Word God gave to us. The Holy Spirit led the people while they wrote the Bible. Many words and ideas are inside the Bible. The words and ideas in the Bible can lead our lives. We can trust the words and ideas in the Bible. The Holy Spirit also helps us understand the Bible when we study it.

He leads to salvation. The Spirit gives people a feeling of guilt about sin. (See John 16:8-11.) The Spirit works to lead people to feel guilty about sin. The Spirit helps people see their need for the righteousness of Christ. People have no hope except in the righteousness of Christ. The Spirit helps people see they will be judged and found guilty if they do not repent.

He lives in the Christian believer. The Holy Spirit comes to live in each believer at the moment the person believes in Jesus. The Holy Spirit does not come into a believer at some time after salvation. The Spirit lives in every believer. (See Rom. 8:9; 1 Cor. 12:3). The Spirit lives in each believer. He leads each believer through life. The Spirit helps the believer follow Christ. The Spirit helps the believer live as Christ lives.

He leads the church. The Book of Acts is called "The Acts of the Apostles." This Book of Acts could be called "The Acts of the Holy Spirit." That name really shows what the Book of Acts is about. Read the Book of Acts. Notice how much the Spirit was working. You will be surprised to see how the Spirit led the church in the Book of Acts. The Holy Spirit leads the work of the church. We need to be open to the way the Spirit leads and to His power. If the church is open to the Spirit, He will show the church what work needs to be done. The Spirit will move the church to help people in the right place and in the right way. The Spirit will lead us to minister where He wants.

In Acts 16, we read that the Spirit would not let Paul go to Bithynia. The Spirit led Paul to go to Macedonia. Later, Paul could look back and see how God was leading. The Spirit led Paul to the place where Paul did most of his ministry. Paul followed where the Spirit led. The Spirit led him to Rome. Paul was a prisoner in Rome. Even as a prisoner, Paul preached about Jesus and wrote many letters that are now in the Bible.

God knows what He is doing. We always need to follow Him, even when we do not understand where He is leading. The Spirit always works to build up the church. The Spirit works to build up each church in each place and to build up the whole church of God in the whole world.

He is our counselor. The Bible says the Holy Spirit is a counselor. (See John 14:16,26.) The Greek language word for *counselor* is *paraclete*. The idea of paraclete is something like a lawyer. The idea of paraclete is the idea of someone who comes to your side to help you. The Holy Spirit is always with the believer. The Spirit helps us through hard times. The Spirit helps us to make our day-to-day decisions. Brother Payne, a mission pastor to a black church in Odessa, Texas, often prayed, "Lord, prop me up on my leaning side." This prayer says in a beautiful way what the word *paraclete* means. The Spirit is at our side to help us.

He is our strength. The believer does not have to do the work of Christ in his own strength. The Holy Spirit gives each believer the power to live for Christ and to serve Him. Some Christians find this out the hard way. Some Christians live and work in their own strength until they are fed up and tired out. These Christians finally find that God's power is there for them. After learning this, these Christians find a new way of life. The power of the Spirit comes at the same time as salvation. It is sad that many Christians do not use this power.

The early Christians were so excited about their faith that one time people thought they were drunk. (See Acts 2:13.) The "Jesus people" of the 1960s and 1970s talked about being "high" on Jesus. To feel great about Jesus on the inside is a wonderful experience. But feeling great may or may not show that a person is filled with the Spirit. The great feeling is not the goal for the Christian. Many Christians who are filled with the Spirit do not feel "high" all the time. The great feeling is not the test of the Spirit's power. The test of the Spirit's power is living with power, joy, and surrender to God.

Part of the work of the Holy Spirit is to help us talk with God. The Spirit leads us in prayer. When we do not know what to say, He explains our feelings that are so deep we do not have clear thoughts about them. (See Rom. 8:26-27.)

He is our teacher. The Holy Spirit does not teach about Himself. The Holy Spirit teaches about Christ. (See 1 Cor. 12:3.) The Spirit is our teacher. He teaches us more about Christ. The Spirit helps us understand who Christ is. The Spirit helps us understand what Christ does. The Spirit helps us know Christ's plan for the world. We can learn more about Christ. Then, we will see the world the way He sees the world. We will give ourselves to be a part of Christ's great work when we see the world the way He sees the world.

The Spirit teaches us how to live the way Christ wants us to live. We learn how Christ feels about sin. We can live more like Christ when we know how He feels about sin. Sometimes the Spirit leads us to work against sins in our society. We may work to get laws passed that protect society's welfare. The Spirit leads us to work against sin by telling people a better way to live.

The Spirit gives spiritual gifts to Christians. Part of His work is to show each of us what gift(s) He gives to us. The Spirit shows us how to use our spiritual gifts for ministry. Many Christians say they do not have spiritual gifts. This is not true. Every believer has spiritual gifts. Every Christian is a minister. Every Christian should work for the Lord.

He is our assurer. The believer will not lose his salvation. Salvation is safe and sure in the Lord. The Holy Spirit helps us understand this promise of salvation. (See 2 Cor. 1:22; 5:5; Eph. 1:14.) Most Christians have times when they doubt their own salvation. Sometimes this is a growing experience. This doubt can be worked out and removed. To know Christ will keep us safe in salvation is a great blessing. The Spirit always helps us know this truth in our lives so we can live in victory.

The Believer's Life in the Spirit

Every Christian has a problem with daily living. Paul talked about this in Romans 7. In verses 1-13 Paul talked about the believer and the Old Testament law. God gave many commandments. God's commandments showed what sin was. The commandments made people feel guilty about their sins. Now we are in Christ. Christians are free from the sinful nature that used to control us. We are also free from the power of the law. We belong to Christ. In Christ we can live to serve God and other people (See vv. 4-6.)

We are in Christ, so we already have victory. However, we still struggle. Now we are believers. God has given us a new nature. At the same time, we still have the sinful nature. Paul talked about his own struggle in verses 14-24. Paul always had this struggle in him. Paul knew the right thing to do. But he often did the wrong thing. (See vv. 15,18,19.) Paul wrote his feeling clearly in verse 20 (GNB): "If I do what I don't want to do, this means that I am no longer the one who does it; instead, it is the sin that lives in me." Paul knew he was responsible for what he did. But, at the same time, he saw the struggle we all face. We will have this struggle as long as we live in this world.

Paul was frustrated and said: "What an unhappy man I am! Who will rescue me from this body that is taking me to death?" (Rom. 7:24, GNB). Then Paul answered his own question: "Thanks be to God, who does this through our Lord Jesus Christ!" (Rom. 7:25, GNB).

Christ has made us free from the power of sin. Paul talked about this in Romans 8. Paul used strong words to say that the Old Testament law could not make us free from sin. The sinful nature cannot obey the law. (See vv. 3-8.) These verses say that trying to follow a long list of do's and don'ts will not give us the power to stop sinning. Some people try to live by following laws. These people have not learned that only Christ can make us free from the power of sin and death. (See vv. 1-2.) Christ gives us power over sin through the Holy Spirit who lives in us. (See vv. 9-11.)

Next, Paul talked about the freedom we have in Christ. This is in the last part of chapter 8. Paul said that in Christ we have the right to call God "Abba, Father." This means we have a new relationship with the Father. (See vv. 14-17.) We can have victory even when we are suffering. We know God is making all things new even when we suffer. (See vv. 18-25.) The Holy Spirit is always with us. He helps us when we are weak. He helps us pray. He prays for us. He gives us strength to stay faithful to the salvation Christ has given us. (See vv. 26-39.)

We must not miss the point of these chapters in Romans. The point is that the Holy Spirit lives in every believer. But many believers live as though they are still in the flesh; following the world. These verses tell us clearly to live in the Spirit. Only in the Spirit can we be free from sin.

Christians must be followers of Christ. One who follows Christ is Christ's disciple. A disciple is a learner and a follower. He is one who wants to be like Jesus. We live a life of discipleship when we live in the power of the Spirit. We can be good disciples when we go where the Spirit leads us. We can be good disciples when we live in the power of the Holy Spirit.

Several things must be in each disciple's life. The Holy Spirit makes it possible for each disciple of Christ to do these several things. The first important thing each follower of Jesus must do to be a good disciple is **pray**. Any believer who feels he/she does not need to pray should study the life of Jesus. Jesus needed to pray, and so do we. Jesus taught us to pray to God as a loving Father. (See Luke 11:2.) Jesus works between us and God when we pray. We can go to God through Jesus because of Jesus' goodness. Jesus is at the Father's right side. He talks to God for us. (See 1 Tim. 2:5; Heb. 1:3; 7:25). We learn even more about prayer. We see the believer has a Father to pray to. We also have a Savior who talks to God for us (intercedes for us). Now we can learn that the Spirit inside of us goes deep into our inner feelings. He aids us when we pray. (See Rom. 8:26-27.)

Hebrews 4:16 is a wonderful verse. It tells us about how a believer can pray. First, the verse says people who believe can go to God in a bold way. The same idea is in Hebrews 10:22 (GNB) which says: "Let us come near to God with a sincere heart and a sure faith." *Boldness* means to go straight, with confidence, in an open way, and without fear. We do not need to be afraid of God.

We are not to go without care or in a light way to God. Yet, because of what Jesus did for us, we are part of God's family. God sees us as beloved children. Some people pray often. Those people find they feel at home with God. They feel comfortable talking with God.

Second, the verse tells us to come to the throne of grace. Jesus, of course, is the King of kings and Lord of lords. Still, we may go to His throne when we pray. He has judged our sins and forgiven us. Jesus said everyone who believes in Him "has eternal life. He will not be judged, but has already passed from death to life" (John 5:24, GNB). Jesus' throne is not a place of judgment but a place of forgiveness. I can go before Jesus in prayer, not as a sinner under the punishment of sin, but as a saved brother with Christ.

Finally, the verse tells us we can go to Him with any need. If we need forgiveness or cleansing or comfort or strength, we can ask for these things. He is there when we need strength, knowledge, or guidance. The Holy Spirit leads us in the wonderful blessing of prayer.

The Holy Spirit leads us to obey. God calls us to obey Him. Someone might think obeying God is like obeying laws. We already saw that obeying laws does not give freedom. Someone might think to obey God is to lose freedom. Many New Testament verses are about obeying God. Many verses show what happens to the person who tries to be free outside of Christ. There is no freedom outside of Christ. People who try to be free by directing their own lives find they are really slaves in sin. They are not free as they thought they were. The greatest freedom comes when we choose to do what God wants us to do.

Hebrews 12:12-29 tells what can happen to a person who does not obey Christ. These verses are about people who are careless. They are not grown up in their spiritual lives. This is opposite from obeying. Jesus always obeyed God. We must obey God's Word that same way. (See John 8:31-32.) We must do what Jesus wants us to do. His will is the law for the Christian life.

Someone might ask, How are we to know what He wants us to do? One answer to that question is, We have the Bible to tell us what He wants. The Holy Spirit led the writing of the Bible. The

Bible leads us to live right. (See 2 Tim. 3:16.) A second answer to the question of how we can know the will of God is, We are led into truth by the Holy Spirit. (See John 14:26.) The Spirit can lead us from inside our lives to understand what God wants us to do. The Spirit gives us power inside to obey God.

The Holy Spirit leads us to find our spiritual gifts. The New Testament teaches that each believer has gifts from the Spirit. Three chapters in the New Testament list spiritual gifts: Romans 12; 1 Corinthians 12; and Ephesians 4. Some of the gifts of the Spirit are in more than one list. These lists do not have all the gifts the Spirit gives. But a study of these lists shows the many different kinds of gifts. The church needs all of God's gifts.

Why do we have spiritual gifts? First Corinthians 12 has a clear answer to that question. Paul wrote to the Christians in Corinth. The Christians in Corinth were proud about their gifts. Paul said that spiritual gifts are for service and ministry, not for pride. (See 1 Cor. 12:4-6.) Also, the Spirit gives spiritual gifts to build up the church. (See 1 Cor. 12:7.) The Bible makes it clear that the Spirit does not give us spiritual gifts so we can feel good or boast.

The Spirit gives each believer a spiritual gift. (See 1 Cor. 12:7.) The Spirit gives some believers more than one gift. These gifts are from the Holy Spirit. The gifts come from the Spirit. He gives the gifts by His own plan. (See 1 Cor. 12:11.) The Spirit can show each person what gift or gifts he has. The Spirit gives us the power to use our gifts for the glory of God and for the good of the church.

The Fruit of the Spirit

We saw how the gifts of the Spirit help the Christian serve the Lord. Now we will see how the fruit of the Spirit gives meaning to Christian living. Galatians 5:22-23 (GNB) tells about the fruit of the Spirit: "The Spirit produces love, joy, peace, patience, kindness, goodness, faithfulness, humility, and self-control. There is no law against such things." In Galatians 5:19-21, Paul listed the acts of the sinful nature. The things in this list are not good. In that list are the worst deeds and feelings people can do and have. There is a great difference between the acts of the sinful nature and the fruit of the Spirit. We see in these verses that evil comes out of human nature. We also see that the great things in the fruit of the spirit come from the Holy Spirit.

We can see another thing when we compare fruit of the Spirit and acts of the sinful nature. There are many wrong acts. But there is just one good fruit. Good comes from one place. Good comes from God. The fruit of the Spirit shows up in several different ways. But, it is all the fruit of the Spirit. We can see that the Spirit can make the good things we saw in Galatians 5:22-23. These good things do not come from the works of people. These good things come from within a person because of the work of the Holy Spirit. This is like the fruit from a good tree.

The fruit of a tree comes from the good life of the tree. That is true for us. If we have the fruit of the Spirit in our lives, they must come from God's Spirit inside of us. The Spirit works inside the Christian. The fruit of the Spirit will show up when the Spirit works inside the Christian.

What does the fruit of the Spirit look like in a person's life? In Galatians 5:22-23, Paul made a list of the characteristics of a life led by the Spirit. The first characteristic is **love**. The Greek language word for love is *agape*. *Agape* is used in the New Testament to talk about God's kind of love. God's love cares for people. God's love will make great sacrifice for people. God's love never stops. (See 1 Cor. 13:8.) God's love wants to save people. It will not give up. People feel love in many different ways. We often use the word *love* without much deep meaning. But the Spirit makes a fruit of *agape* in believers. This kind of love is not normal for us. This love does not come from our own human nature. This kind of love is made inside of us by the Holy Spirit.

The second characteristics of life that the Spirit makes in us is joy. The Greek language word is *chara*. This word is almost the same as the Greek word *charis*. *Charis* is the same as the English word *grace*. This joy from the Spirit is not just a short time of feeling happy. Joy is a gift that makes in us a feeling of goodwill, kindness, and gladness. This joy makes me glad to forgive other people. It helps me overcome some of the worst problems. This joy is a gladness that will never quit. The Holy Spirit alone can make this joy inside of us. I have seen Christians with this joy during the hardest times. This joy is not made by human power.

This joy cannot be stopped by human problems.

The third characteristic of the fruit of the Spirit is **peace**. *Peace* is from the Greek language word *eirene*. This Greek word means full well-being. This peace comes to people who have a right relationship with God and with other people. This fruit of the Spirit does not stop all problems and difficulties for Christians. This fruit is not a way to get away from trouble. This peace is a guard for the heart and the mind that is greater than anyone can understand. (See Phil. 4:7.) This is the peace promised by Jesus. The world cannot give this peace. This peace wins over trouble and fear. (See John 14:27.)

The next characteristic of the fruit of the Spirit is **patience**. The Greek language word is *makrothumia*. This word has the idea of being under self-control. This word does not mean that a person just stands still and takes any pain that comes. This word does not mean that a person just gives up without hope. This patience works toward a goal. The Holy Spirit makes this patience within Christians. Life with patience has a good purpose. We can with patience do many things in life.

Kindness is also a characteristics of the fruit of the Spirit. The Greek language word is *chrestotes*. This word means goodness, honesty, and kindness. Jesus had this kindness. Only the Holy Spirit can make Christians kind like Jesus.

Goodness is from the Greek language word *agathosune*. Paul used this word in Romans 15:14 when he said the Roman Christians were "full of goodness." *Goodness* means righteousness and kindness, as well as goodness. The idea in this goodness is that it is not a quiet characteristic. It is active. This is a goodness that does good things. The Spirit gives this goodness as the fruit of the Spirit.

Another characteristic made by the Spirit in the Christian is **faithfulness**. The Greek language word is *pistis*. This word can mean faith or faithfulness. In this verse, it is better to understand the word to mean faithfulness. Faithfulness comes from a strong active faith. Paul is a good example of this faithfulness. Paul had a strong faith in the Lord. Paul stayed faithful all of his life. We can see how Paul was faithful through his many years of ministry.

When Paul said good-bye to his friends in Ephesus, he showed faithfulness: "I reckon my own life to be worth nothing to me; I only want to complete my mission and finish the work that the Lord Jesus gave me" (Acts 20:24, GNB). Paul had a strong faith in Jesus. He stayed faithful. The Spirit gives this fruit to Christians so we may serve Jesus, no matter what happens in the future.

Gentleness (humility) is from the Greek language word *prautes*. Sometimes the English word *meek* is used to explain this Greek word. In Matthew 5:5 (KJV) *meek* is used in: "Blessed are the meek, for they shall inherit the earth." This word was used to talk about Jesus when He said, "I am gentle and humble in spirit" (Matt. 11:29, GNB). Gentleness is like a person who is modest and courteous. The gentle person will not be proud and boastful. The gentle person will think about himself in the right way. He will be kind to other people. Gentleness is not weakness. Really, there is great strength in gentleness. The Holy Spirit makes gentleness in the lives of believers.

The last characteristic from the fruit of the Spirit is **self-control**. The Greek language word is *egkrateia*. Sometimes the English word *temperance* is used for this Greek word. Self-control is more than temperance. Self-control has the idea of mastering oneself. We should not think this means to be quiet and take whatever happens. Paul understood self-control to mean life under the control of Christ (See Gal. 2:20.) This is the life that is well controlled. The Spirit makes it possible for Christians to live like this.

When Paul finished listing the gifts of the Spirit, he added, "There is no law against such things" (Gal. 5:23, GNB). Of course, there can be no law against this kind of living. We must remember that these characteristics of life are the kind Jesus had. We should remember people hated him and worked against him. Paul did not mean Christians controlled by the Spirit will not have anyone against them. Paul said this kind of living is right and good. No wrong can be found with Christlike living.

The fruit is "of the Spirit." It is from God. It is not made by human work but by the Holy Spirit's wonderful power. Believers need to let the Spirit control them.

PERSONAL LEARNING ACTIVITY 8

We have seen that the fruit of the Spirit are not made by human power but by the Spirit's power. This is like the fruit from a good tree comes from inside the tree. On the tree below, list the characteristics of the fruit of the Spirit found in Galatians 5:22-23. Under each fruit write another word that means the same thing as the name of the fruit.

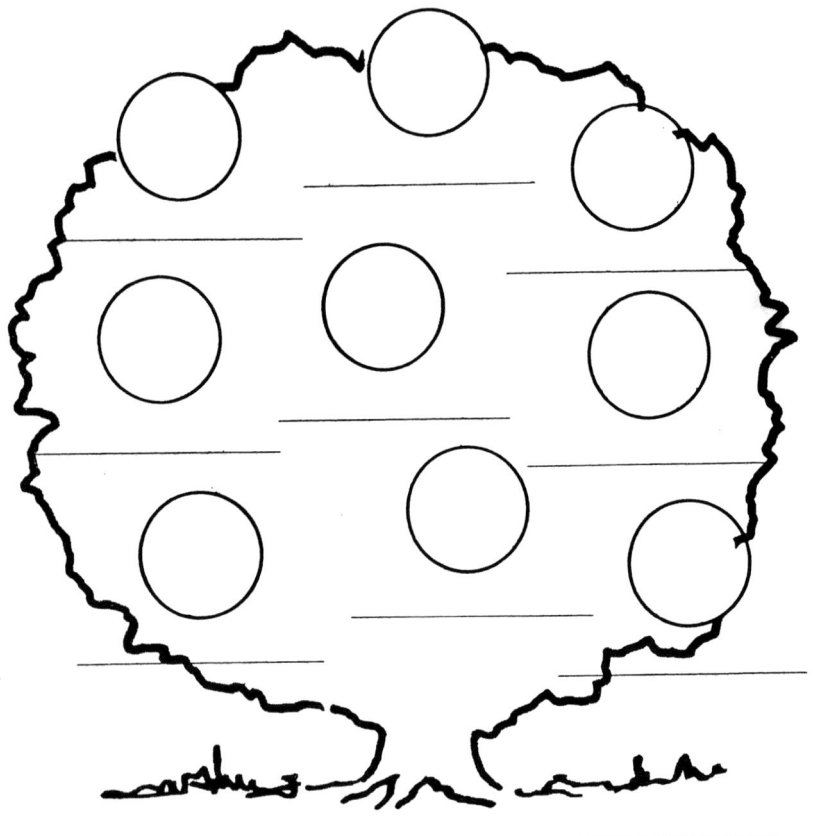

---

[1] W. H. Griffith Thomas, *The Holy Spirit of God* (Grand Rapids: Wm. B. Eerdmans Publishing Company, 1955), 144.

CHAPTER 9

The Church

Simon Peter answered, "You are the Messiah, the Son of the living God." "Good for you, Simon son of John!" answered Jesus. "For this truth did not come to you from any human being, but it was given to you directly by my Father in heaven. And so I tell you, Peter: you are a rock, and on this rock foundation I will build my church, and not even death will ever be able to overcome it."
Matthew 16:16-18, GNB

A really great thing happened at a place called Caesarea Philippi. It was one of the greatest things in all history. Jesus asked His followers the question "Who do people say the Son of Man is?" (Matt. 16:13, GNB). The disciples gave some different answers: John the Baptist, Elijah, Jeremiah, one of the prophets. Many people had different ideas about who Jesus was. People everywhere were talking about Jesus. Then Jesus asked the really important question: "What about you? Who do you say I am?" (Matt. 16:15, GNB). Peter gave an answer for the group. He said, "You are the Messiah, the Son of the living God" (Matt. 16:16, GNB). We often call Peter's words the great confession. When we read the Bible, we see this was the first time the disciples said openly that Jesus was the Christ.

Jesus answered Peter with much excitement: "Good for you, Simon son of John! For this truth did not come to you from any human being, but it was given to you directly by my Father in heaven. And so I tell you, Peter, you are a rock, and on this rock foundation I will build my church, and not even death will ever be able to overcome it" (Matt. 16:17-18, GNB). This is the first time Jesus talked about His church.

The word *church* is the English word for the Greek language word *ekklesia*. *Ekklesia* is used more than 100 times in the New Testament. It means a group of people meeting together for some reason. When Jesus lived, this word was sometimes used to talk about a government meeting in a Roman city-state. The word in the New Testament talks about people called out by God to worship and serve Christ.

Jesus said He would build His church on this rock. What did Jesus mean by *this rock?* (See Matt. 16:18.) Christians have thought a lot about this question. Some Christians think Peter is the rock on which Jesus builds His church. Baptists and other Protestant Christians do not think this is the right way to explain Jesus' words. Some Christians think Jesus was using the words that sound alike but have different meanings.

The Greek word for Peter's name is *petros. Petros* really means a small stone used for building. When Jesus said He would build His church on a rock, He used the word *petra. Petra* really means a large rock like the side of a cliff or a large rock used in the foundation of a building. If this is what Jesus was saying, then Jesus meant He Himself was the foundation stone on which the church is built. Peter and the other believers are the smaller stones that make up the church. One problem with this way to explain the meaning is that the Aramaic language does not have these two different words. If Jesus was speaking Aramaic (Aramaic was the common language for Jewish people when Jesus lived) when He said these things, then He could not have used these two different words.

A better way to understand what Jesus said is to look at the confession of Peter. Peter said that Jesus was the Christ. We should understand that this confession is the rock on which Jesus would build His church. Jesus is the Son of God. The church is built on this fact. People who accept that Jesus is the Son of God are the people who make up the church.

Jesus said that He would build His church. This is important. The church is His, not ours. We must never forget that the church belongs to Jesus.

The Church: Local and Universal

Local and *universal* are hard words. We will see what they mean in the words below. *The Baptist Faith and Message* by Herschel H. Hobbs talks about the church. It says: "A New Testament church of the Lord Jesus Christ is a local body of baptized believers who are associated by covenant in the faith and fellowship of the gospel." Later, *The Baptist Faith and Message* says: "The New Testament speaks also of the church as the body of Christ which includes all of the redeemed of all the ages."

The New Testament uses the word *church* in two different ways. Herschel H. Hobbs shows that the New Testament uses the word *church* 93 times to talk about a church in one place. This is called a *local* church. A *local* church means a church in one place like in the city of Rome or a church in the city of Corinth. This means that most of the verses in the New Testament that use the word *church* are talking about a local group of Christians who meet, worship, and serve in the name of Jesus Christ.

The only time we can see a church is when it is a church in one place under the lordship of Christ. The New Testament never uses the word *church* to mean a church denomination (like Baptist or Methodist or Catholic) or a group of churches. It is really not right to talk about "the Baptist church" if you mean the whole Baptist denomination. The New Testament talks about a group of churches. When it talks about a group of churches, the New Testament always uses the plural "churches" not the singular "church." (See Gal. 1:2.)

The New Testament uses the word *church* to mean a local church most of the time. But, we need to see that the New Testament also used the word to mean a *universal* church. Jesus said, "I will build my church" (Matt. 16:18, GNB). Here Jesus is using the word *church* to mean more than just one church in one place. We can see the same kind of things in Ephesians 5:25, GNB. Here the verse says, "Husbands, love your wives just as Christ loved the church and gave his life for it." Jesus gave Himself for the whole church, which is more than just one church in one place. These two verses show the word *church* can mean all Christians. All believers of all time are part of the church talked about in these two verses. All Christians are brothers and sisters—no matter where they live, what color their skins may be, or what church denominations they join.

The Church: A Believer's Church

Luke wrote the Book of Acts to tell how God worked in the early days of the church. Acts 2:42-47 gives Luke's picture about the earliest days of the Jerusalem church. Verse 47 (GNB) is important saying, "The Lord added to their group those who were being saved." Did you see that the verse says the Lord was adding people to the church? Did you see who was added to the church? Those who were saved (who believed) were added to the church. Acts 2:38 shows that those people who believed were then baptized. We should learn from this that the church is made up only of those who believe in Jesus Christ. Only believers are part of that whole great church of God. Only believers are right people to become members of a local church. Only people who believe are people who should be baptized. We can see this truth also in the story about Philip and the Ethiopian. Only after the Ethiopian believed did Philip baptize him. (See Acts 8:36-37.)

Babies should not be baptized. Babies should not be members in a church. A person is saved by an act of faith in Jesus. One person cannot make a faith decision for another person. Faith does not work that way. One person has faith. My faith does not count in place of your own faith. No one is a believer unless he decides himself to believe. We Baptists have always thought that the church is made up only of believers. So we have always thought that baptism was not right for babies. We cannot make decisions about faith in Christ for other people in our families.

We talk about *believer's church.* When we say *believer's church*, we do not mean that the church belongs to one believer. When we say *believers' church*, we mean that the church is a group of people and all of those people are believers. This group of believers make an agreement together. We say they make a covenant together. This means that each member of the church agrees (covenants) with God and with the other members of the church to live following the beliefs, ways of life, and mission work of that church. Sometimes we are so eager to get people to trust Jesus that we forget to tell people about the covenant idea in a church. We sometimes do not explain about the church to new believers. We need to start new members' classes or find some other way to fix this problem. Churches need to find again that feeling of a group of believers in agreement together.

We Baptists get our idea about a church as a group of people in agreement (covenant) together from the idea of the priesthood of the believer. W. A. Criswell (*The Doctrine of the Church*, pp. 46-47) makes this idea clear. What he said is good and worth quoting. (Paraphrased)

Despite the diversity [differences] in gifts and functions, the church is one body, and all its members have the same relationship to Christ. Access to God's presence was once the exclusive privilege [only the right] of priests. It still is. But the change is that believers are made priests unto God and enjoy direct access through Christ's death and resurrection (Rom. 5:1-2; Rev.1:5-6) so that priesthood now includes all believers . . .

The belief that every believer is a priest is functional in Baptist worship services, church government, and ministry. One is asked to "lead the congregation in prayer"; thus, the congregation prays for all the requests. As many members as possible participate in the services, and the whole congregation normally sings and reads the Bible together as an act of corporate [whole group] worship . . .

Every member shares in the formulation [making] of policies for the local church so that it is not subject to the authority of any external body.

The Church: Biblical Pictures

The Bible uses many different ways to explain what the church is like. We can understand about the church better if we look at the different ways the Bible explains about the church.

The church is the body of Christ. God made the human body. The human body is wonderful. If you think about the human body, you will feel awe (inspired). Paul often compared the church with the human body. (See 1 Cor. 12:12-27; Eph. 1:22-23; 2:16; 4:4,12,16; 5:23,30; Col. 1:18,24; 2:19; 3:15.)

Bill J. Leonard wrote a book named *The Nature of the Church* (Broadman Press, 1986). In that book (pp. 46-47), Leonard said that it is important, for several reasons, to see that the church is the body of Christ.

1. If the church is the body of Christ, then we must understand that Christ is present in the life of His church. This means that there is a real relationship between Christ and the church.

2. Since the church is the body of Christ, the church is united. The human body is united (joined together) as one body. The church also united (joined together) in one body. (See 1 Cor. 12:12.) All Christians are in Christ's body. So we can see that all Christians are joined with all other Christians.

3. Christ is the head of His body. He is the head of the church. (See Col. 1:18.) Christ is the head of the church. He leads the church and joins it together.

The human body works best when all the parts of the body work right. In the same way, the church works best when all the different people in the church work together right. (See 1 Cor. 12:21,24-25.) This helps us see that all the different parts do different things. All of them are still joined into one body. We call this unity in diversity. Paul made it clear that our unity in Christ is more important than anything that can separate us. Paul said that we cannot think about Christians as "Jew and Gentiles, between slaves and free men, between men and women; you are all one in union with Christ Jesus" (Gal. 3:28, GNB).

The church is referred to as the people of God. Two verses in the Bible that show this idea are 1 Peter 2:9-10 (GNB): "You are the chosen race, the King's priest, the holy nation, God's own people, chosen to proclaim the wonderful acts of God, who called you out of darkness into his own marvelous light. At one time you were not God's people, but now you are his people; at one time you did not know God's mercy, but now you have received his mercy."

The church as the people of God looks back to an Old Testament idea. The Old Testament often spoke about Israel as the people of God. The church is God's new people. Because the church is the people of God, the church belongs to God and must do His work in the world. God is building His people into a spiritual house. We, the people of God, must serve God by giving ourselves to Him. We must be a spiritual sacrifice. (See 1 Pet. 2:5.)

The church is called the family of believers or members of God's household. This idea gives us a picture of the church like a family. The people of the church are related to God as Father. The people of the church are related to one another as brothers and sisters. God is our loving Father. (See Gal. 4:6-7.) We are His children. (See Rom. 8:16-17.) We are brothers and sisters in Christ. Because we are brothers and sisters, we must love one another. (See 1 John 3:11.)

The church is the bride of Christ. (See 2 Cor. 11:2; Rev. 19:7-9; 21:9; 22:17.) The church as the bride of Christ is a wonderful idea. This idea makes us think of Jesus' love and care for His church. Ephesians 5:22-32 seems to have this idea. Paul told husbands to love their wives as Christ loved the church. Revelation 19:7-9 tells about a future marriage feast for Christ and His church at the end of time. This is a real picture of great victory and joy.

The kingdom of God is seen in the church. The Bible talks much about the kingdom of God. The kingdom of God is the rule of Christ in the hearts of people. We will see God's kingdom in heaven. Everyone in heaven has given his life to God. The church is God's kingdom on earth. Everyone [each Christian] in the church has given his life to Christ's rule. This idea sees that Jesus is King. He rules over His people. Also, this idea sees that Christians really belong to God's kingdom. His kingdom is more important than any kingdom on earth. (See Col. 1:13.) The Model of Prayer (Matt. 6:9-13), after telling us to praise God, tells us to pray that God's kingdom will come on earth as it is in heaven.

The Church: Ordinances

Baptists call baptism and the Lord's Supper *ordinances*. The word *ordinance* means something which has been ordained, decided, or put in place. Baptists believe that Jesus gave two ordinances to the church—baptism and the Lord's Supper. Baptists do not believe that baptism and the Lord's Supper are sacraments. The word *sacrament* means something that gives grace and salvation. Some people believe that baptism and the Lord's Supper help make someone become saved. Baptists do not believe this.

The ordinances of baptism and the Lord's Supper are important parts of Baptists' life. The Jews used water to make themselves clean for worship. The Jews also used water to baptize people who were not Jews but converted to the Jewish religion. People who became Jews were baptized to show that they were clean and ready to serve God. The Old Testament does not talk about this kind of baptism. However, some other Jewish writings show that Jews used this special baptism when Jesus was alive. John the Baptist used this Jewish baptism. He added another idea to it. John preached that people must become spiritually clean by repenting from sin. John said that the Jews needed to prepare for the coming of God's kingdom by repentance and baptism. John said that first a person must repent and then become baptized. Baptism showed openly that a person had already decided to repent. (See Matt. 3:1-6.)

Jesus was baptized. Matthew 3:13-17 shows that baptism is important. Why was Jesus baptized? Jesus said He must be baptized to fulfill all righteousness. What does that mean? (1) Jesus was baptized to show the world that He was like us. He was a person. (2) Jesus was baptized to be an example. Christians follow the example of Jesus and are baptized. (3) Jesus was baptized to show He was beginning His new ministry. (4) Jesus was baptized to show that His work was related to John's work. John preached that the kingdom was coming. Jesus was baptized to show that the kingdom John had preached about had now come in Jesus. Also, we should see that repentance was important in Jesus' preaching just as in John's preaching. Jesus showed that salvation always includes repentance.

Some people say that Baptists think baptism is not important. They say this because Baptists do not think baptism helps a person become saved. But, we must say clearly that baptism is important for Baptists. It is clear that Jesus commanded believers to be baptized. We must see that everyone who is saved will obey the first command that the Lord gave to us.

Baptism is like a picture. Really, we can see several pictures in baptism. (1) Baptism is a picture of the death, burial, and resurrection of Christ. (2) Baptism is a picture of how the believer has died to sin and been raised by God to a new life in Christ. (3) Baptism is a picture of our joining with Christ. We are baptized under the water in the name of God the Father, Son, and Holy Spirit. This shows our new life in Christ. (See Rom. 6:4; Gal. 3:27.) (4) Baptism pictures that we are joined with the people of God. (See 1 Cor. 12:13.) When a believer becomes baptized, he shows through baptism that he believes that Christ has given him a new life. (See Col. 2:12.) When baptized, a believer shows that he is joined to Christ and joined to the church (the people of God.)

Baptism shows those four things talked about above. We can see that baptism is only meaningful for someone who understands what baptism means. Baptists believe that only believers can be baptized. Baptism does not help a baby in any way. Baptism does no good for a young child who is not old enough to understand about sin. A baby, or any young child who is not old enough to understand about sin, is put under the water or sprinkled with water. That baby or child is not baptized. The baby or child gets wet, but he is not baptized. A person must first have an understanding faith in Jesus Christ as Lord. Then, the person can be baptized.

Baptists also strongly hold this idea that going under the water (immersion) is the only right way to be baptized. We find our belief in the Bible. The Greek language word *baptizo* means immersion, or to go under the water. *Baptizo* has no other meaning. Also, only going under the water shows the right picture of the death, burial, and resurrection of Christ. Only going under the water shows the picture of dying to sin, being buried, and rising to new life.

Baptists will not give up their belief that baptism means going under the water. Some Baptist churches make a rule that Christians from other denominations who want to join a Baptist church must be baptized by immersion (going under the water). Some churches make this rule even if the person joining the church feels he has already been baptized. Most Baptist churches will accept believers as members if the church the new member comes from believes the same as Baptists about baptism. Several other denominations believe the same as Southern Baptists about immersion.

We agree that baptism is not needed for a person to be saved. Someone might ask, Why make such strict rules about baptism if it is not needed for salvation? The reason for the strict rules is that the idea (doctrine) about baptism is important and needs to be kept clear. Baptism is only for believers. Baptism is only by going under the water (immersion). Baptism is not needed for salvation. Baptism is an ordinance for the church and not for one person. We must hold on to these ideas or the doctrine of baptism, as the Bible teaches it, will be lost.

Baptists also have the ordinance of the Lord's Supper. Sometimes we call this ordinance *communion. Communion* means to be with someone in fellowship. It almost has the idea of talking (communicating) with someone. Paul wrote a letter to the Corinthians and said: "The cup we use in the Lord's Supper and for which we give thanks to God: when we drink from it, we are sharing in the blood of Christ. And the bread we break: when we eat it, we are sharing in the body of Christ" (1 Cor. 10:16, GNB). You can see in this verse the idea of fellowship or being together with Christ (communal emphasis).

It is really better to call the Lord's Supper a Memorial Supper. All four of the Gospels tell the story of Jesus starting the ordinance of the Supper. (See Matt. 26:26-29; Mark 14:22-25; Luke 22:17-20; less clearly in John 13.) Also 1 Corinthians 11:23-25 has the story. The story tells clearly that the reason for the Supper is to remind Jesus' followers for all time about Jesus' death on the cross. The *bread* reminds us of Jesus' body that was broken for us. The *cup* reminds us of Jesus' blood that was given for us. We must continue having the Lord's Supper until Jesus comes back.

Jesus gave us the Lord's Supper. The Jews in the Old Testament had the Passover. The Lord's Supper and Passover are like each other in some ways. Jesus helped us see that the two are alike when He started the first Lord's Supper at the Passover time of year. The Jews used the Passover to remember how they got away from Egypt. The Lord's Supper reminds us of how we got away from sin.

Who can take the Lord's Supper in Baptist churches? Baptists have different ideas about this. Some Baptist churches think that when a church has the Lord's Supper that only members of that church should take the Supper. This idea is from the Landmark way of doing things. Most people who think this way say that a church can only control its own members. So, they say only local members should take the Lord's Supper.

Some Baptist churches let anyone who is a member of any Baptist church take the Supper. Some Baptist churches let anyone take the Supper who comes from a church which holds believer's baptism. Many Baptist churches let all believers in Christ take the Lord's Supper. The main rule for who can take the Supper is faith in Christ. Paul said to the Corinthian church, "Everyone should examine himself first, and then eat the bread and drink from the cup" (1 Cor. 11:28, GNB). If a church lets any believer take the Supper, that means the church wants each believer to examine himself.

There is no rule about how often a church should have the Lord's Supper. Some churches take the Supper once each month. Some churches take the Supper once every three months. Some churches take the Supper only a few times each year. The Bible does not tell us how often to take the Supper. We should take the Supper often enough that we always remember what Christ did for us. We should not take the Supper so often that we forget how important it is. The Lord's Supper is best when the whole worship service is used for the Supper. This way the Supper is a time to remember and also a time when lost people may accept the Lord.

The Church: Offices and Ministries

The Baptist Faith and Message talks about two offices of the church. The word *office*, here, does not mean a room to work in. The word *office* means a special position of work in the church. The two church offices are pastor and deacon. Pastor and deacon are two special jobs in the church. We call them church offices. Southern Baptists have tried to give a lot of attention to all the people of the church. We use the word *laity* to mean all the people of the church. Southern Baptists have studied the doctrine of the laity in the past. We have given attention to the laity with different programs like Shared Ministry. The Year of the Laity, finding spiritual gifts, and other ways. We have tried to give strong attention to the work by laypeople in the church. Baptists have always given much attention to the work of the laypeople in the church. But we also need to see that the pastor and the deacon have important work in the church. We will now talk about the work of the pastor and the deacon.

The pastor is the leader of the church. Many verses in the New Testament show this. (See 1 Tim. 5:17-19; 1 Pet. 5:1-5.) It is clear that the pastor is the leader. We need to ask what kind of leader the pastor will be. Ephesians 4:11-12 gives us the answer. Those verses say that the pastor (and the apostles, prophets, and evangelists) must help God's people get ready to serve the Lord.

Sometimes we use the word *equip* to mean helping God's people get ready to serve the Lord. We say the pastor must equip God's people. Different pastors will have different ways to equip the people. But whatever way the pastor uses, the pastor must always have the goal to equip the people for service.

The pastor is not the "boss." The pastor leads the church because the church lets him lead. As the leader, he is always under the church in authority. The pastor should lead in a humble way. He should always pray for God to help him. He should live like Christ. Then the people will respect him. The pastor is the leader of the church.

The Bible does not show the work of the deacon as clearly as it shows the work of the pastor. *Deacon* is the English word that comes from the Greek language word *diakonos*. *Diakonos* means servant. The work of the deacon slowly changed during New Testament times. We do not know exactly what the deacons did back then. Maybe the deacons at first did not have exact responsibility. Maybe the deacons did whatever needed to be done, each deacon doing what he had gifts to do.

Some people think that the first verses about deacons are Acts 6:1-6. This is the story about seven men chosen by the church. These men had the responsibility to make sure the Greek-speaking widows in the church who needed food were not ignored. The word *deacon* is not used in this story. Many people think that the office of deacon started from that time. We do know that by late in the New Testament time churches were using deacons and pastors. (See Phil. 1:1; 1 Tim. 3:1-13.)

Now we do not know exactly what the deacons were supposed to do. The word *deacon* helps us some. *Deacon* means to serve; to do ministry. The New Testament does not support the idea that deacons are like a board of directors. A board of directors controls a business. Deacons do not have control over the church. Deacons must be spiritually grown up (mature). Each church picks its own deacons. The deacons must lead in the church and serve in ministry. If deacons take control of a church, they are not following the Bible example for deacons. Deacons can serve in many ways. They may help plan for the church or counsel people with problems. They may advise the pastor or other people with needs. They support the things the church does. They live as a good example to other people.

A Baptist church does many things. The pastor and the deacons cannot do all the things in a church. Many people must be willing to help minister. These are volunteer ministers in the church. Some of these volunteer ministers will teach, lead, work in Sunday School or Discipleship Training. Some of these volunteer ministers will do music, missions, and committee work. Some churches will have many people working for the church. These workers are on staff. They are paid for their work. Each church is responsible to use the gifts that the people have. Jesus is the judge over every church. Each member in a church must find his gifts and use those gifts for service in ministry. The church has the responsibility to let the members use their gifts. The church must help the members (equip the members), so each member can minister better. When every member is working right and faithfully, the church can reach out in many ways to a lost world.

The Church: Purposes of the Church
The church belongs to Jesus. The church is in the world to do His work. What is the church like? What must the church do? If we understand Jesus' work, then we will understand what the church

is like and what the church must do. We will now take a look at some of the things the church does.

Worship is the most important thing the church does. Walter T. Conner (in *The Gospel of Redemption*) wrote, "The first business, then, of a church is not evangelism, nor missions, nor benevolence; it is worship." (Broadman, p. 277). Conner explained that worship leads the church in all it does. When the people worship, they praise and listen to Christ. After praising and listening, the people know what Christ wants them to do. Southern Baptists have many programs to help the church. We can have many programs and have good worship. We must be careful that worship services do not become only times for advertising our programs. We must worship God in a right way.

The right way of worship involves the whole person. We must worship God with our minds and with our feelings. When we worship, we praise God for who He is and what He has done. When we worship like this, we will learn and know more about God. Read the verses in Revelation that talk about what happens around God's throne. Those verses show us that God made us to worship Him.

Proclamation is another thing the church does. *Proclamation* means to tell out or to preach. Before Jesus left the earth, He told His disciples: "But when the Holy Spirit comes upon you, you will be filled with power, and you will be witnesses for me in Jerusalem, in all of Judea and Samaria, and to the ends of the earth" (Acts 1:8, GNB). This verse and the verses in Matthew 28:18-20 are called the Great Commission. Jesus gave this Commission (or command to work) to His church. We must preach and tell out the gospel to all peoples in all the world. We do not have a choice about this. Proclaiming the gospel is what the church must be doing.

There are at least five things involved with fulfilling the Great Commission. The first part to fulfill the Great Commission is witnessing. God's plan is that the people who have accepted His love and have believed on Jesus will live for Jesus. Part of living for Jesus is telling people the story of faith in Jesus. (See Acts 5:32.)

The second part to fulfill the Great Commission is that we

must care for people with their needs. We must see people as Jesus saw them. Jesus looked at people with deep love. He saw them as sheep without a shepherd. (See Matt. 9:36.) We must care deeply for people. Then we can be good witnesses.

The third part to fulfill the Great Commission has to do with the places of mission. Jesus cares for all people. Jesus wants us to care for all people. There is no line on the map where Jesus' care stops. He wants us to go every place where people live.

The fourth part to fulfill the Great Commission is power. Jesus sends us with power. Jesus promised His followers, "When the Holy Spirit comes upon you, you will be filled with power" (Acts 1:8, GNB). When we proclaim His word with power, we know that the word will change things. This story is a good example of this power.

Mary Slessor was a young girl from Scotland. She went to Africa as a missionary many years ago. She worked with men most of the time. She was trying to reach the different African people for Jesus. One day she told a chief who had become a Christian: "Here is what God wants us to do. He wants us to take this whole tribe for Christ. Then He wants us to go to the next tribe, and tribe by tribe God wants us to spread over Africa. My prayer is we will reach Africa for Christ out of this tribe that has come first to know Christ."

The chief listened to her plans and replied: "You can't do all of that. You are only a woman." She said, "Yes, I am only a woman, but have you forgotten what kind of God this woman has?"

The final part to fulfill the Great Commission is that we must speak as we go. Jesus gave this command to His disciples, "Go, then, to all people everywhere and make them my disciples" (Matt. 28:19, GNB). If we make a word-for-word translation from the Greek language to English, that verse would look like this: "Going, therefore, disciple all the nations." The idea is that we must witness as we go. This job for Christian is so important that we cannot wait for the perfect time.

Keith Parks is the president of the Foreign Mission Board. Parks tells this story about when he was a missionary in Indonesia. He lived on a big road that was still a dirt road. The dust from the road was bad. One day the wind was blowing the dust away from his house, so he was studying his Bible near the road. He saw many people walking down the road. He decided to count the people. He tried but he could not count fast enough. He saw all those many people. He became burdened for those many lost people. He cried out to God: "God, you have sent us here. My wife and I are the only missionaries in this area. God, how can we reach these many people?"

God gave him an answer. "One at a time, Keith, one at a time." Keith Parks got up from his knees. He went out to the road to look for that one. He saw a woman in the road who had dropped her things. People were walking on her things in the road. Parks went into the crowd of people. He started helping the woman pick up her things. He said to her: "Mother, you're hot and tired. Will you come into my yard and sit down and have something cool to drink?" He carried her things and led her to the yard.

She asked him: "Sir, why did you do that? Why did you get down in the dirt and help pick up my things? Why did you give me a cool drink and a place to rest?"

Parks answered, "I am so glad you asked me that." He went on to tell her about Jesus. She did accept Christ as her Savior. God's way is one at a time. God's time and place are whenever and wherever we have the chance to share the gospel.

Discipleship is an important thing for every church. *Discipleship* means to learn to be a better follower of Christ. The Great Commission tells us to lead people to Christ. It also tells us to make disciples. (See Matt. 28:19-20.) A disciple is someone who is learning from Jesus. Disciples learn and also follow Jesus. Disciples grow in what they know. They also give their lives to Jesus more and more. Disciples also find their spiritual gifts. They become more willing to use their gifts in ministry.

The church helps Christian disciples. The church has Bible study and times for training. Also, the church helps people become involved in ministry. Christians are always growing as disciples. The church must always be helping them grow. We use Discipleship Training as a program to help Christians grow as disciples. The goal for churches is to help Christians grow to be mature. Churches want Christian disciples who have the right beliefs. Churches want Christian disciples who can serve Christ through the church.

Fellowship is a big thing for every church. The Greek language word for fellowship is *koinonia*. This word is used many times in the New Testament. The New Testament says that believers have fellowship with one another, with Christ, and through the Spirit. This word shows that the church is a fellowship of believers. These believers are held together by the Spirit. Jesus Christ is the foundation for this fellowship.

A man named Ken Lyle tells a story about when he and his family lived in New York City. His little girl was playing at a playground with a fence all the way around it. Soon it was time for the little girl to come in. But when Ken's wife looked for the girl, she was gone. The wife called Ken. He went home to help look for the girl. Some people who lived near helped look, too. Finally, they called the police. After a long time, they heard the girl coming up the stairs into their house. They wanted to spank the girl and hug her at the same time. They asked her, "Where have you been?"

She answered: "I have been helping Kathy. The head came off her doll, and I helped her try to put the head back on. We couldn't get it on, so I have been helping Kathy cry."

We can't always help Christian friends solve their problems. But in the fellowship of the church, when we cannot help solve a problem we can be with those friends to help them cry.

PERSONAL LEARNING ACTIVITY 9

When Jesus talked about the church, He called it "my church." Christ owns the church. What does it mean if Christ owns the church? Answer the questions below. Think about what it means if Christ own the church.

1. If we see that Christ owns the church, how will that influence the way the church worships?

_____

_____

_____

2. If we see that Christ owns the church, how will that influence the things the church does?

_____

_____

_____

3. If we see that Christ owns the church, what will we say are the most important things for the church?

_____

_____

_____

_____

CHAPTER 10

Last Things

Then I saw a new heaven and a new earth. The first heaven and the first earth disappeared, and the sea vanished. And I saw the Holy City, the new Jerusalem, coming down out of heaven from God, prepared and ready, like a bride dressed to meet her husband. I heard a loud voice speaking from the throne: "Now God's home is with mankind! He will live with them, and they shall be his people. God himself will be with them, and he will be their God. He will wipe away all tears from their eyes. There will be no more death, no more grief or crying or pain. The old things have disappeared."
Revelation 21:1-4, GNB

The Bible shows that history is going toward God's goal. History does not go in circles. Things do not happen over and over again forever. History is not getting better by itself. No, history is moving in the way God wants. History will go where God has planned.

Christians study about where God is leading history. We study about what will happen at the end of history. We say we are studying *last things*. This means we are studying what will happen at the end of history. Sometimes we say we study *eschatology*. *Eschatology* is just a big word that means last things.

Last Things are important. This is an important doctrine for Christians. But Christians have different ideas about what will happen at the end of history. Many Christians really study the Bible and really love the Lord. Yet, these Christians will have different ideas about Last Things. Baptists feel it is all right for Christians to have different ideas about Last Things. We do not test other Christians about Last Things and refuse to fellowship with other Christians if they do not agree with us. Christians do have different ideas about the end of history, but all Christians believe God is working in history. All Christians believe Jesus will come again. Christians believe we will be with Jesus in heaven. Revelation 11:15 (GNB) shows the goal of history in a beautiful way: "The power to rule over the world belongs now to our Lord and His Messiah, and He will rule forever and ever!"

Now we will study Last Things. We will see several important truths in these few pages.

Last Things: Death and the Time Before Jesus Returns

Jesus will come again. Some people will meet God face to face at that time. Most people will meet God when they die. Many people refuse to think about death. People who understand that they will die often change the way they live to be ready for death.

Christians need to think about what we believe about death. Christians have different ideas about death than people who are not Christians. Christians sometimes compare death to birth.

When a baby is born, it is not easy. The baby is comfortable inside the mother. Inside the mother is the only place the baby has known. The baby does not want to leave its comfortable place. To be born is painful. The baby does not want to be hurt. When the baby comes into the world outside the mother, it finds a big world. The world is so big that the baby will use all its life learning about the world. As the child grows, it will find love and joy and many other feelings that will make life good.

Christians are not in a hurry to go through death. Sickness leading to death is often painful. We do not know much about what happens after death. This world is comfortable. This is the world we know. When we pass through death, we are born into a new world much greater than earthly life. This is just like the idea of the baby born into this world. After death, we are with the Lord. We have a life free from sin and sadness. We have full love and joy and many other wonderful things to make our lives great.

Christians also believe the body will rise from the grave. We believe in resurrection. (See 1 Cor. 15.) One question that bothers many people is, What happens to the Christian between the time of his death and the resurrection of his body at the end of time? People give different answers to this question. I will talk about two answers that some people give that are not in the Bible.

One idea not in the Bible is that the soul sleeps before the resurrection. The people who think this way believe that after the body dies the soul is sleeping until the resurrection. People try to support this idea with verses like 1 Thessalonians 4:13 (KJV), which says that dead believers are "those who are asleep." The New Testament does not support the idea of soul sleeping. Herschel H. Hobbs says that *sleep* in this verse is "a synonym [word that means the same thing] for death as a cessation [stopping] of labor, sorrow, and trouble." (See *A Layman's Handbook of Christian Doctrine*, p. 51.)

Another idea not in the Bible is purgatory. Some people believe in purgatory. They think purgatory is a place where Christians go after they die. Christians in purgatory are getting ready for heaven. These people think Christians are made pure in purgatory. Purgatory is a place for people who are saved but are not yet perfect. In purgatory people get forgiveness for remaining sin. This idea is not in the Bible. There is no support for this idea in the Old Testament or in the New Testament.

These two answers are not good enough. We must look more to answer what happens to Christians between the time of death and the time of final resurrection.

Ray Summers wrote a book named *The Life Beyond* (Broadman Press). Summers said he likes the word *disembodied* to explain the time after death and before the resurrection of the body. The word *disembodied* means outside the body, or without a body. People often use the words *intermediate state* to explain the time between death and resurrection. *Intermediate* means between. So the words *intermediate state* mean the time between death and resurrection. Summers likes the word *disembodied* better than the words *intermediate state*. He thinks some wrong ideas come from the words *intermediate state*. (See pp. 18-19.)

We all know that when the body dies it goes back to the earth. The body becomes dirt. During the time the body is dirt, we are *disembodied.* Summers explains the disembodied time as "the conscious existence of both the righteous and the wicked after death and prior to the resurrection."(See pp. 18-19.) These hard words mean that the disembodied time is the time between death and resurrection when the mind still knows what is happening even though the body is dead. Saved people and sinners both know what is happening even though their bodies have died.

Christians are with the Lord between death and resurrection. Paul said this in 2 Corinthians 5:6,8 (GNB). Paul said, "So we are always full of courage. We know that as long as we are at home in the body we are away from the Lord's home. We are full of courage and would much prefer to leave our home in the body and be at home with the Lord." When a Christian dies, he or she is "at home" with the Lord. The old body is dead. The Christian will get a new resurrected body. The Bible makes that promise. But in the meantime, the Christian is with the Lord.

Believers die and go to be with the Lord. Sometimes the Bible says that believers are in paradise. Jesus promised the thief on the cross that he would be with Jesus in paradise. Jesus said that the thief would be with Him on that same day. (See Luke 23:43). The word *paradise* is used in two other New Testament verses. In 2 Corinthians 12:4 (GNB), Paul told a story about when he was "snatched to Paradise." Revelation 2:7 (KJV) promises: "To him that overcometh will I give to eat of the tree of life, which is in the midst of the paradise of God."

Many people agree that the word *paradise* comes from the Persian language. *Paradise* means a beautiful garden or park. It might mean a park near the king's house. The Bible uses the word *paradise* to mean the presence of God. The idea here is that when Christians die, they go to be with God in paradise. Christians in paradise are with God—blessed, at rest, and in joy.

Ray Summers explains what the Bible says about people who die trusting Jesus. (1) They still know what is happening (conscious). These people are alive and aware in the presence of God. (2) After death, their relationship to God does not change. The Bible does not have any idea about people having a second chance to change their mind after death. There is no idea in the Bible about purgatory for a time of cleansing. Each person decides before death what to do with God's salvation. After death, that decision cannot be changed. (3) Those who die trusting Jesus will get a resurrected body in the future. We learn from the Bible that man is body and spirit. We will get a resurrected body. Then redemption will be complete. (See *The Life Beyond,* pp. 23-24.)

What happens to people who die without faith in Jesus Christ? What happens to those people between death and the last judgment? We can see that when these people die their bodies go back to dirt. What happens to their souls?

Some people think people who do not have faith in Jesus will die and their souls will be destroyed. They think the soul of a nonbeliever is forever dead. This idea is not in the Bible. Baptists do not believe it.

The Bible says everyone who dies—Christian or non-Christian—goes into hades. *Hades* is a Greek language word. The Hebrew language word that means the same thing is *sheol.* Both of these words mean the place of the dead. The King James Version of the Bible changes these words to the English word *hell.* This is not fully a right translation. *Hades* has the idea of the place for all the dead and not just the place where dead people are punished. There is a place for all the dead. This is the idea of *hades.* The New Testament makes it clear that the place for the dead in Christ is heaven and the place for the dead without Christ is hell.

Luke 16:19-31 is the story about the rich man and Lazarus. Many people know this story. Both men died. Lazarus was carried to Abraham's side. (See v. 22.) There he was comforted. (See v. 25.) We can see that Lazarus knew what was happening; and he was at rest, in comfort, and joy. Lazarus had the experience of a saved person in paradise. (The word *paradise* is not used in this story.)

The rich man had a fully different experience. The rich man went to hades. Hades was a place of great pain for the rich man. He knew about his pain. He cried out for just a drop of water to make his pain less. (See vv. 23-24.) He could not get what he wanted. There was no way to go between the place of Lazarus's peace and the place of the rich man's pain. Abraham answered the rich man by saying: "There is a deep pit lying between us, so that those who want to cross over from here to you cannot do so, nor can anyone cross over to us from where you are" (Luke 16:26, GNB).

Peter wrote in 2 Peter 2:9 (GNB) "The Lord knows how to rescue godly people from their trials and how to keep the wicked under punishment for the Day of Judgment." Ray Summers (in *The Life Beyond*) writes about this verse and says, "This indicates [means] that the unrighteous [lost people] enter immediately into a state of punishment and that they experience that punishment until the time of final judgment (p. 25).

People who die without faith in Jesus suffer punishment between the time of death and the final judgment. But this time of suffering is not their final hell. Ray Summers ends his writing about the punishment of sinners between the time of death and the final judgment (p. 29) with three important ideas. (1) People without faith in Christ know what is happening after they die. (2) After death, their relationship with God does not change. Remember that Abraham told the rich man in Luke 16 that his situation could not be changed. (3) People who die without faith in Christ will still experience the resurrection, final judgment, and hell.

We can see the time between death and the resurrection is a time when Christians experience joy. We can also see that the time between death and the final judgment is a time when people who do not have faith in Jesus will experience punishment. When we die, we will experience one or the other of these things.

Last Things: the Resurrection of the Body
John 5:25 (GNB) has Jesus' words: "I am telling you the truth: the time is coming—the time has already come—when the dead will hear the voice of the Son of God, and those who hear it will come to life." Later Jesus said, "Do not be surprised at this; the time is coming when all the dead will hear his voice and come out of their graves: those who have done good will rise and live, and those who have done evil will rise and be condemned" (John

5:28-29, GNB).

The Bible clearly teaches about the resurrection. We have already seen that people who die are now in paradise or in punishment. But humans will not be disembodied forever. Everyone will be raised from the dead.

The New Testament has many verses that talk about the resurrection. We can find verses about the resurrection in Matthew, Mark, Luke, and John. Also, there are verses about the resurrection in Acts, Paul's letters, and in Revelation. Paul wrote about the resurrection in 1 Corinthians 15. That chapter makes it clear that the doctrine of the resurrection is important for the Christian faith. Paul said several things about the resurrection. (1) He said that many people saw Jesus after He rose from death (See 1 Cor. 15:3-8.) (2) Because Jesus rose from the dead, believers know that God will raise them from death. (See vv. 20-22.) (3) Paul showed that if there is no resurrection of the body, then we must see that God did not raise Jesus either. If God did not raise Jesus, then our faith is no good and useless. (See vv. 12-19.)

We believe God will raise us with new bodies from death. This idea helps us see that life continues. When God raises our bodies, then life is fulfilled. We know that eternal life begins when a person is born again (saved). At that time, the believer starts a new life in Christ. Yes, the believer has a new life; but the believer is still in this world. The believer is still tempted, and the believer is still weak. It is normal that the believer sees death and has fear. But the believer knows there is life after death.

If Christians understand about the resurrection, then they can go through times when other people hurt them because they are Christians. Christians can die for Christ. They know death is not the end. We know this is true. This knowledge about resurrection gives us real strength in life. We can live the way God wants us to live even if His way is different from the world's way. We can follow God, no matter what happens.

The Christians in Corinth had a hard time understanding what kind of body Christians would have after the resurrection. Many Christians today worry about that same thing. You might think, *If the body changes to dirt and goes back to nature, how can God raise it?* Paul answered that by saying that resurrection does not mean we will have exactly the same flesh-and-blood body we have now. (See vv. 35-44.) We cannot compare our natural body with the resurrection body. All we know is that God Himself will make a body for each Christian that will be just right.

The body will be a perfect resurrection body. It is not important how God will fix the body. It is important for us to see that we will not be spirits without bodies. It is also important to see that our spirits will not be lost in some great all-including spirit. Each Christian will be a real person. Each Christian will be himself or herself. Each Christian will have his own personality. The body that God gives us in resurrection will not get old. It will not die. It will not pass away. (See 1 Cor. 15:53-54; Rev. 21:4.)

We can know more about the resurrected body by seeing what the Bible says about Jesus' resurrected body. John said that we will be like Him (1 John 3:2). Jesus had a body after His resurrection. The disciples saw Jesus. They knew Jesus. (See Luke 24:36-43; John 20:19-20,24-29.) The disciples could touch Jesus. (See John 20:27.) They could eat with Him. (See John 21:10-14.) We can also see that Jesus' body was different in some ways. Jesus could disappear while the disciples were looking at Him. (See Luke 24:31.) Jesus could appear in a room even though the doors were locked. (See John 20:19.) Our resurrected body will be as Jesus' is.

Many people want to know when the resurrection will happen. Paul gave us some answers in 1 Corinthians 15:51-52 (GNB): "Listen to this secret truth: we shall not all die, but when the last trumpet sounds, we shall all be changed in an instant, as quickly as the blinking of an eye. For when the trumpet sounds, the dead will be raised, never to die again, and we shall all be changed."

Other verses tell us the trumpet will sound when Jesus comes back. When Jesus comes back, God raises the believers who have already died. Believers who are still alive when Jesus comes back are changed. We can see that all of God's people will have new bodies that cannot die again. Death is finished forever. All of God's people will have this great victory. (See 1 Cor. 15:53-56.)

God will also raise people who are not Christians. Many verses in the Bible tell us this. We can see this idea in these verses: Daniel 12:2; Acts 24:15; Revelation 20:12-13; and John 5:18-

29. You may ask, When will the resurrection of people who are not Christians happen? Many Christians believe that the resurrection of lost and saved people will happen at the same time. These people believe when Jesus comes again everyone will be raised.

Other Christians think the Bible talks about two different resurrections. These Christians believe Christians will be raised when Jesus comes again. But these people think persons who are not Christians will be raised after Jesus has ruled on earth for 1,000 years. This rule of Jesus is called the millennium. (*Millennium* means 1,000.) People who have this idea find support in verses like Revelation 20:4-6 and 1 Thessalonians 4:13-18.

Last Things: Christ's Second Coming

There are several different ideas about Christ's second coming. All Southern Baptists do not hold to the same idea. Some Southern Baptists have one idea; others have different ideas. Southern Baptists have always agreed that Jesus really will come again and start a new heaven and earth. We have never required that everyone hold the same idea about Jesus' second coming. Through all the years of Christian history, several main ideas about His return have been developed. Some Southern Baptists hold to each of these different views.

The different views about Jesus' return are all called millennial views. These views are called *millennial* because each different view refers to different ideas that Christians have about the millennium. The word *millennium* is not in the Bible. *Millennium* is a Latin language word that means 1,000. Revelation 20:2-7 talks about a 1,000-year rule of Christ. This is where the idea about a millennium comes from.

The different ideas about Jesus' return are named: premillennium, postmillennium, and amillennium. *Pre* means before; so, premillennium is the idea that Christ will return before the 1,000-year rule. *Post* means after, so postmillennium is the idea that Christ will return after the 1,000-year rule. *A* on the front of a word means no, so, amillennium is the idea that there is no real 1,000-year rule of Christ but that the millennium is a symbol. People who have this idea say the millennium is a symbol for the time from when Christ left earth until the time He comes back again. The premillennial idea is divided again into two kinds of premillennium views. These two premillennium views are like each other in some ways and different from each other in other ways.

Today, not many people hold the postmillennium idea. Many people held this idea before World War I. This idea about the millennium says that through strong evangelism and mission work the world will be won to Christ. This view thinks that Jesus will rule in the hearts of believers. Because Jesus rules in so many believers' hearts, He will be ruling the world. This idea holds that Christ's rule will begin this way and continue for 1,000 years. At the end of the 1,000 years, Satan will try to fight with his army against God. This idea says that Satan will be beaten and Christ will start a new heaven and a new earth. B. H. Carroll was the man who started Southwestern Baptist Theological Seminary. Carroll believed strongly in this view.

Many Southern Baptists today hold the amillennial view. People who hold the amillennial view say that the ideas in Revelation and in some of the prophet books are symbols. A *symbol* is a word or a picture or an idea that stands for something else. An example of a symbol for Americans is the bald eagle. When an American sees the picture of a bald eagle, he will think about America. The bald eagle is a symbol for America. People who hold the amillennium idea think that the millennium is a symbol for God's rule in the hearts of believers. These people think that when we read about a 1,000-year rule of Christ, we should understand that to be a symbol for Christ ruling in the hearts of believers.

Some people say that amillennialists do not believe that Christ will really return. It is wrong to say that about amillennialists. People who hold the amillennial view do believe that Christ will come again. The amillennial view says that Christ can come at any time. This view does not believe that anything else must happen first. Christ could come now. Augustine lived about 400 years after Jesus. Augustine was the first person to write about this idea. The amillennial view was the idea that most Christians had from the time of Augustine until the Protestant Reformation in the 16th century. Today, Southern Baptists such as Ray Summers and Herschel Hobbs hold this view.

There are two different premillennial views. One of these views is called the historical premillennial view. The other premillennial view is called the dispensational premillennial view. First, we will look at the historical view. Then, we will look at the dispensational view.

The historical premillennial view sees the book of Revelation in almost the same way as Christians saw it between the time of the New Testament and Augustine. The historical premillennial view thinks that God's people will become stronger and stronger. This view also thinks the work of Satan will grow. There will be a person who is fully against Christ at the end of time. This person is called the Antichrist. *Antichrist* means against Christ.

The Antichrist will trick the world. Many people will follow him. Christians will be badly punished by the Antichrist and his followers during this time. This view says that during this time God will use the Jews in some way the Bible does not explain. But, the Jews will be saved by grace through faith just as Gentiles (people who are not Jews) are saved.

The historical premillennial view says there will be 7 years of terrible trouble (tribulation) for the church. Christ will come again at the end of the 7 years. Believers will rise to meet Him in the air. At that time, Christ will beat Satan in a war called the battle of Armageddon. (Armageddon is the name of a valley in Israel.) Christ will start a rule of 1,000 years on earth after Satan is beaten. This view says that at the end of the 1,000 years Satan will get his army together for one last fight against God. Satan will be beaten again. The judgment comes after this. Then God will start a new heaven and a new earth.

Many people who have this historical premillennial idea think the numbers in Revelation are symbols and do not limit the length of time. For example, they may think that the No. 7 or the No. 1,000 might be a symbol and not mean only 7 years or only 1,000 years. The people who hold the historical premillennial view believe that all the things listed (coming of Antichrist, time of tribulation, return of Christ, rule of Christ, and so on) will come true.

People who hold the dispensational premillennial view believe history is divided into several different times. These different times are called *dispensations*. This view thinks God worked in different ways during each dispensation. I will give you some examples of the different dispensations. This view says that the first dispensation was the time before Israel started. The second dispensation was the time when Israel was a nation. Other dispensations are times like the church age and the time of the millennial kingdom. This view is hard to explain in an easy way. Also, not all dispensational premillennialists agree fully with one another about everything. This view agrees with the historical premillennial view on some things. For example, both views agree about the coming of the Antichrist, the time of great trouble (tribulation), the war at Armageddon, the 1,000-year rule of Christ, the battle after the 1,000-year rule of Christ, the judgment, and the new heaven and earth.

We can also see that the historical premillennial view and the dispensational premillennial view explain prophecy in different ways. Because these 2 views have different opinions about prophecy, they find different answers in the verses that have prophecy. One example is in chapter 2 and 3 of the Book of Revelation. There are 7 letters to 7 churches in those 2 chapters.

The dispensational premillennial view says the 7 letters are not only letters to 7 churches in the past. This view says that each letter shows us 1 of the 7 church ages. This view says that right now we are in the last church age, the age when many people turn away from Christ (apostasy).

People who hold the dispensational premillennial view feel that the nation of Israel will start again because it is still the people God chose. Also, Christ will come back to earth part of the way; and the true church will be called up (raptured) to meet Christ in the air. This view says that this is the start of the time of great trouble (tribulation).

The dispensational premillennial view does not think that Christians will go through this time of great trouble. During the time of great trouble, the Christians will be judged. After they have been judged, each Christian will get a job to do during the coming 1,000-year rule of Christ (the millennial kingdom). During the first half of the time of great trouble (tribulation), the Jews will be tricked and will help the Antichrist. Then the Jews will see their mistake and will turn to God. When the Jews turn to God, a time of terrible trouble will come on the Jews. However, many Jews will join the kingdom and come to Christ. At the end of the time of great trouble, Christ will come back to earth. He will start the 1,000-year rule as king. Christ will rule the world as a powerful king. He will rule through the Jewish nation in Jerusalem. Christ will use the Christians who had different jobs given to them after their time of judgment.

The people who believe the dispensational premillennial view see the end of the 1,000-year rule almost the same way as the historical premillennialists. However, the people who hold dispensational premillennial views think there will be several resurrections and several judgments. The dispensational premillennial view started in the 19th century. The Plymouth Brethren in England were the first people to start this view. Many people in the United States accepted this view. The ideas of dispensational premillennialism were spread through many Bible meetings and through the Scofield Reference Bible. Many Southern Baptists hold this view.

We can see that there are many different views about these things. The one part that is really needed for faith that comes from the Bible is the belief that Christ really will come again. *The Baptist Faith and Message* does not make a clear statement about how Christ will return. That is what the writers wanted. *The Baptist Faith and Message* says one thing very clearly—**Christ will come again.**

There is no doubt Christ will come again. The Bible says this clearly. (See John 14:28; Acts 1:10-11; 1 Thess. 4:16.) This thought, that Jesus will come again, has often helped Christians in times of trouble. We need to have a good understanding about this belief. When we truly believe Jesus is coming again, we will work hard to bring other people to Christ. Also, when we understand that Jesus is really coming again, we will live the way Christ wants us to live. Many times Christians will not agree about the coming of Christ. Still, we need to study what God has shown us about Christ's coming again.

Last Things: Judgment and Eternal Destiny

The Bible tells us that God wants to save all people. God has always been trying to call people to come to Him. But when the end time comes, there will be a judgment. In chapter 2, we saw that God is judge. Here, we must see that everyone will be judged by God. (See Rev. 20:12-13.) Everyone must go through the judgment—Christians and people who are not Christians. We know the Christian is safe in the blood of Christ.

Christians must stand before God and explain to God about their faithfulness. (See Rom. 14:10-12; 2 Cor. 5:10.) We give weak excuses today for not serving God first in our lives. Our excuses seem to be good reasons to us. When we stand before God, we will see what is really important. People who never trusted in Jesus will be afraid before God. God will tell every time they had a chance to repent but they did not repent. When God judges them guilty, everyone will see that God's judgment is right.

The Bible does not tell us much about heaven. But, the Bible does tell us some things about heaven. The Bible tells us that heaven is real. It is a place of wonderful glory. Here are some things the Bible says about heaven:

1. Heaven is a real place. (See John 14:2.)
2. Jesus will be there in heaven. (See John 14:3.)
3. God will be there in heaven. (See Rev. 21:22-23.)
4. There will be no sin or suffering in heaven. Heaven will be pure. (See Rev. 21:4,27; 22:1-3)
5. We will have different kinds of rewards in heaven. Our reward will follow our faithfulness. (See Matt. 25:14-30.)
6. In heaven we will know things and understand things. (See 1 Cor. 13:8-12.)
7. In heaven we will always praise God with great joy. (See Rev. 5:11-13; 15:2-4.)

The Bible also talks about hell. We find the word *hell* in the King James Bible. There are really three different Greek language words and one Hebrew language word that are put into English by the one word *hell*. The Hebrew language word *sheol* and the two Greek language words *hades* and *tartarus* really mean death or the place of the dead. We find a clear idea about hell in the New Testament.

The Greek language word *gehenna* is also put into English with the word *hell*. This word means hell—the place of punishment. *Gehenna* was the garbage dump in the Hinnom Valley just south of Jerusalem. This dump was always on fire. Everyone hated this place. It was used as a place for worshiping false gods during the time of the Hebrew kings. Some of the kings had worshiped false gods in that valley. They had sacrificed their children to the false gods. (See 2 Chron. 28:1-3; 33:1-6.)

Josiah was a good king. Josiah helped the Hebrew people come back to God. Josiah made that valley the city dump. Dead animals and the bodies of dead criminals were thrown into the dump. So, the word *gehenna* means a hated place—always burning. The Bible uses that word *gehenna* to explain hell. Because the Bible uses that word for hell, we should see clearly that hell is a real place where some people will suffer forever. Hell is a real place, even if some people do not think so.

Jesus talked about this hell several times. (See Matt. 5:22,29-30; 18:9; 23:15; Mark 9:43-47; Luke 12:5.) The Book of Revelation says that hell is a lake of fire. (See 20:14-15.) Jesus said that hell is a place where "the worms that eat them never die, and the fire that burns them is never put out" (Mark 9:48, GNB). Many kinds of trash were put in the gehenna dump. Maggots grew there all the time. Maggots are tiny worms that become flies when they are adults. The fire never stopped burning at the gehenna dump. The words *never put out* come from the Greek language word *asbeston*. The English word *asbestos* comes from the Greek word *asbeston*. The idea in this word is something that can be put in fire but it is not burned up. This word helps us see that the punishment of hell keeps on going.

Jesus said many other things about hell. You can find His words in Matthew 10:28; 13:41-42,49-50; 23:33; 25:41,46; Luke 16:22-23; John 5:28-29. John (in the Book of Revelation) calls hell "the lake of fire" (Rev. 20:15, GNB). If you look at all these words about hell, you will get a terrible picture in your mind of a place of burning that never stops—a lake of fire.

It makes good sense to believe in hell if we believe in life after death. If there is a place of joy and rest for God's faithful people, then there is a hell for people who refuse God. The Bible shows this clearly. The writer of Daniel said, "Many of those who have died will live again: some will enjoy eternal life; and some will suffer, some to everlasting life, and some to shame and eternal disgrace" (Dan. 12:2, GNB).

We all understand the idea of justice. The right thing must be done. Now, people who break the law and people who hurt others are put in prison. They are separated from people who obey the law. This separation is needed for the good of all people and to protect people. This is the idea of justice. After this life is over, there will still be justice. It makes good sense that God's justice will be fulfilled in heaven and hell. It makes good sense to see there is a hell.

People who refuse to follow God and refuse His mercy are living in rebellion against God. These people are not right for the goodness and purity of heaven. The Bible teaches that sin destroys people's lives. Sin sends them to hell. Yes, God loves these people very much. But these people have rejected God's love. Because they reject God's love, they condemn themselves to hell.

Last Things: a New Heaven and Earth

History will end when the world passes away and a new heaven and a new earth are made by the Lord. (See Rev. 21:1.) We do not know what all this means. We do not know exactly what a new heaven and a new earth mean for us. We do not know exactly what a new heaven and a new earth mean for the world God has made. The Bible does help us see how wonderful the new heaven and new earth will be. Second Peter 3:13 tells us to wait for it with great expectation. Paul used exciting words to talk about it. Paul said all God had made would be set free. He said the world was like a person waiting for a baby to be born. The world is waiting like one in childbirth until that time. Paul says we cannot imagine what we will be. (See Rom. 8:18-22.)

Paul explained the coming of the new heaven and earth in 1 Corinthians 15:24-28. Paul said Christ would beat every enemy. Even death will be beaten. Then Christ will give the kingdom to His Father. This is the last part of the full story of salvation for

Christians. This is the last thing that happens in the kingdom of Christ.

Walter T. Conner (in *The Gospel of Redemption*) wrote, "It is not to be something unrelated to, or out of line with, what he did in founding that kingdom" (pp. 326-327). Conner also explained that Jesus' second coming does not mean that Jesus left this world and did not do anything in this world until He comes again. We must see that He rules now from heaven. He is working to move history toward the time when this age will end.

The Sermon on the Mount explains the perfect way for people to live together. That is how we will live in the new heaven and earth. We work towards a world like that now, but we will only have such a life in the end. Only saved people will be in this new place of God, and God Himself will be its light.

When I was 17, I sat with my mother when she died. She spoke. I did not understand what she said. I asked her what she was saying. She spoke again. She said, "I see Jesus." She lifted her hand like she was waving to someone. Then she died. She had a look of peace and joy on her face. Jesus promises, "After I go and prepare a place for you, I will come back and take you to myself, so that you will be where I am" (John 14:3, GNB).

Christians know God takes care of the future. Some of us may go to meet Him when we die. Some of us may see Him when He comes again. All Christians know we are in His hands.

PERSONAL LEARNING ACTIVITY 10

Different Christians have different ideas about how Jesus will come again. We saw four different ideas in this chapter. Give a short explanation for each view listed below. If you need help to remember, look back in this chapter. Draw a circle around the view that is most like your own idea of Jesus' second coming.

Postmillennialism: ⎯⎯⎯⎯⎯⎯⎯⎯⎯⎯⎯⎯⎯⎯⎯⎯⎯⎯⎯⎯

⎯⎯⎯⎯⎯⎯⎯⎯⎯⎯⎯⎯⎯⎯⎯⎯⎯⎯⎯⎯⎯⎯⎯⎯⎯⎯⎯⎯⎯⎯⎯⎯

Amillennialism: _____

_____

Historical premillennialism: _____

_____

Dispensational premillennialism: _____

_____

Teaching Guide

Introduction

This teaching guide contains detailed teaching plans to assist you in leading a group study of *The Doctrines Baptists Believe.* The plans can be used with either a large or a small group.

The teaching plans in this guide are self-contained—that is, they enable you to lead good sessions without additional resources. However, *The Doctrines Baptists Believe—Teaching Workbook* is highly recommended. The teaching workbook contains a supply of overhead cel masters, worksheet masters, teaching posters, and discussion cards. These resources provide visual aids to enrich the sessions and other tools to involve group members actively in the learning process. Group size is no problem. The resources are effective with large auditorium groups and with small groups in classrooms. Only one copy of the teaching workbook is needed. The cel masters, worksheet masters, posters, and discussion cards may be reproduced. Suggestions for using all of the resources are included in the teaching workbook.

Learning Goals
Upon completion of this course, each group member should have a better understanding of a number of the doctrines Baptists believe and their implications for his or her life. Each session has a specific learning goal related to this general goal. The learning goals will help you maintain a focus as you lead the sessions.

Planning Actions
1. Nothing can substitute for study and prayer. Pray for the guidance of the Holy Spirit as you prepare for and lead the sessions.

In addition to this book and *The Doctrines Baptists Believe—*

Teaching Workbook, two tapes are available: a BTN videotape, *The Doctrines Baptist Believe,* and a Broadman audiocassette tape by the same title. Both tapes by William H. Stephens are designed to give you, the leader, background and supplementary information on the doctrines.

2. Encourage the participants to read the appropriate chapters in *The Doctrines Baptists Believe* in preparation for each session.

3. Prepare a poster outline of the session titles to use in all of the sessions. Prepare a 1 by 4 arrow pointer from poster board and glue the arrow to a clothespin. Use this pointer with the outline poster.

THE DOCTRINES BAPTISTS BELIEVE

Session 1: The Bible: the Inspired Word of God
The Doctrine of God
(Chapters 1 and 2)
Session 2: In God's Image
The Doctrine of Christ
(Chapters 3 and 4)
Session 3: The Atoning Work of Christ
The Doctrine of Salvation
(Chapters 5 and 6)
Session 4: The Christian Life: Priests of God
The Christian Life: Living in the Spirit
(Chapters 7 and 8)
Session 5: The Church
Last Things
(Chapters 9 and 10)

4. The ideas for the teaching posters in each session of this guide are taken from *The Doctrines Baptists Believe—Teaching Workbook.*

5. If you have a large number of persons in the study, small-group work can be handled easily. Simply divide into as many small groups as necessary to involve everyone. The same assignment can be given to more than 1 small group. For example, if the teaching plan calls for 5 small groups to be given 5 assignments and 100 persons are in the study, form 25 small groups.

Five groups would be given the first assignment, 5 groups the second assignment, and so on.

6. Make extensive use of the Bible as you teach. It is the textbook for studying the doctrines Baptists believe. The Bible alone is our authority for faith and practice.

7. Use your imagination in preparing for and leading the sessions. Do not feel bound by the suggestions in this guide.

8. Begin and close each session with prayer.

9. Following each session, spend some time evaluating the session. Think of ways you can improve future sessions.

10. The following hymn was written especially for this doctrine study. A stanza is devoted to each of the 10 chapters in the book. You may want your group to sing the appropriate stanza as you teach each chapter.

THE DOCTRINES BAPTISTS BELIEVE

William H. Stephens

Sing to the tune of the hymn "Lord, Send a Revival."

1. God's Holy Word, what a joy to read;
His direct voice, it's my only creed.
Witness to Jesus, inspired, each word;
Deeply my soul is stirred.
O witnessing, truthful Word;
O pow'rful, compelling Word;
O gift of revealing God;
By Holy Spirit heard.

2. Sov'reign Creator, Almighty God;
Mountains and valleys Your foot has trod.
Awesome and holy we hold Your name;
Yet to our midst You came!
O e'er-present, caring Lord;
O all-knowing, loving Lord;
O all-pow-rful, saving Lord;
I raise to You this hymn.

3. Favored of God, man creation's goal;
   Image of Him: spirit, mind, and soul.
   Once walked with God, sinful, fallen race;
   Blind, depraved, and base.
   O thinking yet scheming ones;
   O free yet rebellious ones;
   O strong yet weakly ones;
   You are in need of grace.

4. Jesus is Prophet, and Priest, and King;
   He is the Ruler of everything.
   Savior, Redeemer, and Lord is He;
   He lived and died for me.
   O human and hurting One;
   O God and eternal One;
   O Christ of the Three in One;
   I give my all to Thee!

5. Emptied Himself, Jesus Christ came down;
   Dwelt among men, gave up heav'n and crown.
   Suffering Servant, He showed His way;
   Then died my price to pay.
   O healing, redeeming Lord;
   O crucified, suff'ring Lord;
   O glorified, risen Lord;
   You conquered death for me!

6. How to be saved people long have sought;
   Turning to Christ, what fierce wars are fought!
   You must repent of your life and will;
   Then confess Christ and yield.
   O what a great joy is He!
   O what purpose, now I'm free!
   O hope clearly now I see!
   Thy presence my life fill.

7. I am a priest by redemption's price;
   No one between God and me save Christ!

High Priest, He rent the veil in twain,
New cov'nant bought in pain!
O ev'ry believer's right!
O truth of the churches' might;
O access to Abba's light!
Lord, we sing this refrain.

8. Minist'ring, serving mankind each day;
Ev'ry believer must show the way,
Led by God's Spirit to lost mankind,
Each dark recess to find.
O holiness is Your call!
O ministry is Your call!
O witnessing is Your call!
We are called soul and mind.

9. Body of Christ, in you He does dwell;
Ne'er to succumb to the gates of hell;
Sinners redeemed held by Christ's strong hand;
Such is this mighty band!
O family of Christ on earth!
O col'ny of heav'n on earth!
O Bride when He comes to earth!
In You we seek to stand.

10. One day I'll cross o'er the stormy sea;
On that far shore Jesus waits for me.
Death, through your womb to eternal life,
End to this world of strife!
O death now where is your sting?
O joyf'lly for heav'n I sing!
O to Jesus' breast I cling!
By His great light I see.

Session 1
The Bible: the Inspired Word of God
The Doctrine of God

(Chapters 1 and 2)

Learning goal: After completing this session, participants should have a better understanding of the doctrines of the Bible and of God. They will be able to: (1) explain in their own words at least four basic beliefs about the Bible and (2) explain in their own words at least four basic beliefs about God.

Before the Session

1. Have copies of *The Doctrines Baptists Believe* available for participants. Have registration materials and a Baptist Doctrine Diploma available.

2. Prepare a copy of the following true/false pretest for each member (or use worksheet 1 in *Teaching Workbook*). (1) The Bible is inspired in the same sense that other great books or poems are inspired. (2) Some parts of the Bible are more inspired than other parts. (3) God is one and has made Himself known as three Persons. (4) Pantheism is the view that God is everywhere at all times. (5) Persons have the freedom to choose between right and wrong. (6) Sin basically is ignorance of the will of God. (7) Jesus Christ is fully divine and also fully human. (8) Jesus rejected the term *Lord* for Himself. (9) The main work of Jesus on earth was to be our example. (10) *Predestination* means that God has predetermined that some persons will be saved and others will be lost. (11) The term *atonement* refers to the reconciling act of God by which He dealt once for all with the sin that separates persons from God. (12) *Regeneration* means *the unmerited favor of God.* (13) All believers have equality before God. (14) Sanctification is a once-for-all act whereby God

declares the sinner justified. (15) Every believer receives the Holy Spirit at the time of conversion. (16) To be filled with the Spirit means to be controlled by the Spirit. (17) The word *church* in the New Testament always refers to a local body of believers. (18) Baptism and the Lord's Supper are sacraments through which the church dispenses grace. (19) The resurrection of the body is not taught in Scripture. (20) All judgment is here in this life.

3. Prepare the following agree/disagree statements (or use worksheet 2 in *Teaching Workbook*). You can write the statements on the chalkboard; you can write them on strips of adding-machine tape and attach the strips to the board or wall; or you can make copies to hand out. (1) Those who insist on the absolute truthfulness and authority of the written Word of God tend to worship the Bible rather than the God who gave it. (2) No person knows exactly how God inspired the writing of Scripture. (3) The criterion by which we interpret the Bible is the church. (4) Creeds have a valid place in Baptist life. (5) The term *Trinity* refers to the succession of ways God has appeared in history. (6) There has never been a time when God did not exist. (7) God has revealed enough of Himself through nature for a person to be saved. (8) The Bible does not reveal why God created the universe.

4. Write the following statements on large sheets of newsprint. "All Scripture is inspired by God" (2 Tim. 3:16, GNB). "The word of our God endures forever" (Isa. 40:8, GNB). The Bible is divine in its origin. When we believe the Word of God, we believe God. The Bible is truth, without any mixture of error. The Bible is a beacon to show wanderers the way to go. The eternal God reveals Himself to us as Father, Son, and Holy Spirit. Wherever we are, at any time, God is there. God has measured "the ocean by handfuls" (Isa. 40:12, GNB). Our Heavenly Father reigns with providential care over His universe. Mount these teaching posters in random order on the walls around the room.

5. Place a small table at the front of the room. Place an open Bible in the center of the table. Also place the following objects on the table: a lamp, a hammer, a jar of honey, a sword or a knife, a loaf of bread, a glass of water, a mirror, and some seeds. Read the following Bible verses related to each symbol: lamp (Ps. 119:105); hammer (Jer. 23:29); honey (Ps. 119:103); sword (Eph. 6:17); bread (Matt. 4:4); water (Eph. 5:26); mirror (Jas. 1:23-25); seed (Luke 8:11).

6. Write the following words on strips of adding-machine tape: One, Spirit, Person, Infinite, Perfect, Creator, and Sovereign.

7. Prepare to speak on chapters 1 and 2, following the outline in the book. However, do *not* plan to lecture nonstop during the session. Plan to make the study a teaching/discussion session.

During the Session

1. Quickly care for administrative matters. Distribute copies of *The Doctrines Baptists Believe.* Show the Baptist Doctrine Diploma and explain how the diploma is earned. Encourage everyone to earn one.

2. Use the outline poster to overview the entire study. Share the general learning goal for the study. Emphasize the importance of doctrine and the need for each person to be well grounded in the basic doctrines of our faith. Then focus on the topics for session 1.

3. Ask volunteers to read aloud the agree-disagree statements. As each statement is read, determine those who agree with the statement, those who disagree, and those who are undecided. If the group is divided into opinion, allow time for discussion of the statement.

4. Lecture on the points in chapter 1. Write the points on the chalkboard as you deal with each one. Allow time for discussion.

5. Call attention to the objects on the table. Ask members to share any Scripture passage that relates each object to the Word of God. Discuss the meaning of each symbol as it relates to the Bible.

6. Lecture and lead a discussion on the points in chapter 2. Mount each word strip (step 6, "Before the Session") to the chalkboard or wall as you discuss it.

7. Call attention to the teaching posters on the walls. Ask volunteers to read the statements and to comment on their meanings.

8. Distribute the pretest and ask members to complete it before the next session by marking the statements T (true) or F (false). (Answers are in session 5.)

Session 2

In God's Image
The Doctrine of Christ

(Chapters 3 and 4)

Learning goal: After completing this session, members should have a better understanding of the doctrine of man and the doctrine of Christ. They will be able to: (1) explain in their own words at least four basic beliefs about the doctrine of man and (2) explain in their own words at least four basic truths about Christ.

Before the Session

1. Write the following outline of chapter 4 on strips of adding-machine tape: (1) The Incarnation of God; (2) Born of a Virgin; (3) The Supreme Revelation; (4) Prophet, Priest, and King; (5) Divine and Human; (6) The Promised Messiah; (7) The High Priest; and (8) Lord and King.

2. Plan to lecture on and lead a discussion of chapter 4. Follow the outline in the book.

3. Prepare the following teaching posters. Mount them in random order on the walls. We are made in the image of God. Persons are the crown of God's creation "All of us were like sheep that were lost" (Isa. 53:6, GNB). Sin is rebellion against God. One of the greatest wastes of all is the waste of human potentiality. (See Rom. 3:23.) Jesus Christ is God. Jesus is greater than anything we can say about Him. Jesus Christ is too big for any definition. "Whoever has seen me has seen the Father" (John 14:9, GNB). "Jesus loves me! This I know."

During the Session

1. Call attention to the outline poster. Focus on session 2. Use Personal Learning Activity 3 as a basis for discussion to create

interest in chapter 3.

2. Divide members into five small groups. Assign each group one of the following points from chapter 3: "In God's Image: Man, the Goal of Creation," "In God's Image: Persons Are Created Free," "Fallen in Sin: the Origin and Nature of Sin," "Fallen in Sin: a Description of Sin," and "Fallen in Sin: the Results of Sin." Ask each group to summarize and explain its assigned topic. Allow time for group work and call for reports.

3. Lecture on and lead a discussion of chapter 4. Mount each word strip (step 1, "Before the Session") to the chalkboard or wall as you lecture.

4. Refer to Personal Learning Activity 4. Lead a discussion based on this activity.

5. Ask volunteers to read the teaching posters and to comment on their meanings.

Session 3
The Atoning Work of Christ
The Doctrine of Salvation
(Chapters 5 and 6)

Learning goal: After completing this session, members should have a better understanding of the atonement and the doctrine of salvation. They will be able to: (1) explain at least four biblical terms related to Christ's atonement; (2) explain the steps involved in salvation; and (3) explain what salvation means to the believer.

Before the Session

1. Plan to lecture on and lead a discussion of chapter 6.

2. Prepare the following agree/disagree statements (or use worksheet 9 in *Teaching Workbook*). (1) *Repentance* involves a change of mind that allows God to change one's heart and life. (2) A person can receive Christ as Savior without accepting Him as Lord. (3) Saving faith does not involve the intellect. (4) The doctrine of the eternal security of the believer means that anyone who joins a church is secure. (5) Jesus did not die as a substitute for us. (6) *Redemption* refers to the deliverance from the bondage and consequences of sin. (7) *Reconciliation* means reformation. (8) The New Testament concept of justice and righteousness is based on keeping the law.

3. Prepare the following teaching posters. Mount them in random order on the walls. The cross is at the very center of the Christian faith. He who knew no sin became the sin bearer for humanity. "God loved the world so much" (John 3:16, GNB). We are redeemed "with the precious blood of Christ" (1 Pet. 1:19, KJV). Christ died in our place. "You must all be born again" (John 3:7, GNB). Faith is trust and obedience. Forsaking All, I Trust Him. Salvation is threefold. Open confession of

Christ speaks to the very nature of faith.

During the Session

1. Refer to the outline poster. Focus on session 3. Use the agree/disagree statements as a basis for discussion.

2. Divide members into four small groups. Assign each group one of the following sets of words: (1) *substitution/covenant;* (2) *sacrifice/redemption;* (3) *reconciliation/justification;* and (4) *propitiation/expiation.* Ask each group to study chapter 5 and to define each of the two assigned terms. Allow time for group work and call for reports.

3. Lecture on the doctrine of salvation, using the outline in the book. Allow time for discussion of the various points.

4. Refer to Personal Learning Activity 6. Call for volunteers to share their testimonies, using the three-point outline.

5. Ask volunteers to read the teaching posters and to comment on their meanings.

Session 4
The Christian Life: Priests of God
The Christian Life: Living in the Spirit

(Chapters 7 and 8)

Learning goal: After completing this session, members should have a better understanding of the Christian life. They will be able to: (1) state three main truths about the doctrine of the priesthood of believers; (2) describe sanctification; and (3) describe the work of the Holy Spirit.

Before the Session

1. Prepare to lecture on and lead a discussion of chapters 7 and 8.

2. Prepare the following agree/disagree statements (or use worksheet 11 in *Teaching Workbook*). (1) Some believers are called into ministry. (2) All believers are priests. (3) The word *sanctification* means without sin. (4) It is possible for a Christian to miss God's will for his or her life. (5) The Holy Spirit is a power or influence radiating from God. (6) The Holy Spirit deals only with Christians. (7) The gifts of the Spirit are the same as the fruit of the Spirit. (8) Every Christian has the fruit of the Spirit.

3. Prepare the following teaching posters. Mount them in random order on the walls. All believers are called by God to ministry. Each of us is a bridge builder. You and I are God's *naos*. Sanctification has three aspects. "I run straight toward the goal" (Phil. 3:14, GNB). "Continue to grow in the grace and knowledge of our Lord and Savior Jesus Christ" (2 Pet. 3:18, GNB). Every believer receives the Holy Spirit at the time of conversion. The Holy Spirit provides the power for the Christian life. Life in the power of the Spirit is a life of discipleship. All of

God's people are gifted.

During the Session

1. Refer to the outline poster and focus on session 4. Use the agree/disagree statements as the basis for discussion.

2. Lecture briefly on chapter 7, following the outline in the book. Allow time for discussion.

3. Refer to Personal Learning Activity 7 and ask volunteers to respond.

4. Lecture briefly on chapter 8 and allow time for discussion. Use the chalkboard to list the work of the Holy Spirit.

5. Refer to Personal Learning Activity 8 and ask members to respond.

6. Ask volunteers to read the teaching posters and to comment on their meanings.

Session 5
The Church
Last Things

(Chapters 9 and 10)

Learning goal: After completing the session, members should have a better understanding of the doctrines of "The Church" and "Last Things." They will be able to: (1) summarize in their own words at least two basic beliefs about "The Church"; (2) explain in their own words the significance of baptism and the Lord's Supper; and (3) explain in their own words at least three biblical truths about "Last Things."

Before the Session

1. Prepare to lecture on and lead a discussion of chapters 9 and 10.

2. Prepare copies of the true/false test used in session 1 to use as a posttest.

3. Prepare the following agree/disagree statements (or use worksheet 14 in *Teaching Workbook*). (1) Simon Peter is the rock on which Christ built the church. (2) All believers of all the ages are part of the universal church. (3) Baptism is essential to salvation. (4) Baptism and the Lord's Supper are local church ordinances. (5) Belief about Last Things is a test of orthodoxy and fellowship in a Baptist church. (6) Eternal life for the believer begins with the second coming of Christ. (7) Only the righteous will be resurrected. (8) All judgment is finished for the believer.

4. Prepare the following teaching posters. Mount them in random order on the walls. " 'On this rock foundation I will build my church' " (Matt. 16:18, GNB). We must never forget that the church belongs to Jesus. The church is a community of

174

believers. We are part of the family of God. History is His story. Death is the time when most people will meet God face to face. A person's destiny is determined by his or her response to Jesus Christ. Those who die without Christ go to a place of punishment. "I will come back" (John 14:3, GNB). Heaven is a prepared place for a prepared people.

During the Session

1. Refer to the outline poster and briefly review the entire study. Then focus on session 5. Use the agree/disagree statements as the basis for discussion.

2. Lecture briefly on chapter 9, following the outline in the book. Allow time for discussion.

3. Refer to Personal Learning Activity 9 and ask members to respond.

4. Lecture briefly on chapter 10, following the outline in the book. Allow time for discussion.

5. Refer to Personal Learning Activity 10 and lead the group to summarize these four views.

6. Ask volunteers to read the teaching posters and to comment on their meanings.

7. Hand out the posttest and allow time for members to complete it. Discuss the answers. Answers: 1. *F*; 2. *F*; 3. *T*; 4. *F*; 5. *T*; 6. *F*; 7. *T*; 8. *F*; 9. *F*; 10. *F*; 11. *T*; 12. *F*; 13. *T*; 14. *F*; 15. *T*; 16. *T*; 17. *F*; 18. *F*; 19. *F*; 20. *F*.

8. Express appreciation to members for their participation in the study. Close by singing a hymn.

The Church Study Course

The Church Study Course is a Southern Baptist education system designed to support the training efforts of local churches. It provides courses, recognition, record keeping, and regular reports for some 20,000 participating churches.

The Church Study Course is characterized by short courses ranging from 2½ to 10 hours in length. They may be studied individually or in groups. With more than 600 courses in 24 subject areas, it offers 130 diploma plans in all areas of church leadership and Christian growth.

Complete details about the Church Study Course system, courses available, and diplomas offered may be found in a current copy of the *Church Study Course Catalog*.

The Church Study Course system is jointly sponsored by many agencies within the Southern Baptist Convention.

How to Request Credit for This Course

This book is the text for course number 05063 in the subject area: "Baptist Doctrine." This course is designed for 5 hours of group study.

Credit for this course may be obtained in two ways:

1. Read the book and attend class sessions. (If you are absent from one or more sessions, complete the "Personal Learning Activities" for the material missed.)

2. Read the book and complete the "Personal Learning Activities." (Written work should be submitted to an appropriate church leader.)

A request for credit may be made on Form 725 "Church Study Course Enrollment/Credit Request" and sent to the Awards Office, Sunday School Board, 127 Ninth Avenue, North, Nashville, Tennessee 37234. The form on the following page may be used to request credit.

A record of awards will be maintained by the Awards Office. Within three months of completion of a course, a copy of the transcript will be sent to the church for distribution.

CHURCH STUDY COURSE
ENROLLMENT/CREDIT REQUEST
FORM · 725 (Rev. 1-89)

MAIL THIS REQUEST TO ▶

CHURCH STUDY COURSE AWARDS OFFICE
BAPTIST SUNDAY SCHOOL BOARD
127 NINTH AVENUE, NORTH
NASHVILLE, TENNESSEE 37234

Is this the first course taken since 1983? ☐ **YES** If yes, or not sure complete all of Section 1. ☐ **NO** If no, complete only bold boxes in Section 1.

SECTION 1 · STUDENT INFO

STUDENT

Name (First, M.I., Last)

☐ Mr. ☐ Mrs. ☐ Miss

Social Security Number | — | — |

Personal CSC Number *

DATE OF BIRTH ▼ | Month | Day | Year |

CHURCH

Church Name

Mailing Address

City, State | Zip Code

Street, Route, or P.O. Box

City, State | Zip Code

SECTION 2 · CHANGE REQUEST ONLY (Current inf. in Section 1)

☐ Former Name

☐ Former Address | Zip Code

☐ Former Church | Zip Code

*CSC # not required for new students. Others please give CSC # when using SS # for the first time. Then, only one ID # is required.

SECTION 3 · COURSE CREDIT REQUEST

Course No.	Title (use exact title)
1. 5890-15	DOCTRINES BAPTIST BELIEVE – BASIC ENGLISH
2.	
3.	
4.	
5.	
6.	

SECTION 4 · DIPLOMA ENROLLMENT

Enter exact diploma title from current Church Study Course catalog. Indicate diploma age group if appropriate. Do not enroll again with each course. When all requirements have been met, the diploma will be mailed to your church. Enrollment in Christian Development Diplomas is automatic. No charge will be made for enrollment or diplomas.

Title of Diploma | Age group or area

Title of Diploma | Age group or area

Title of Diploma | Age group or area

Signature of Pastor, Teacher, or Other Church Leader | Date